ENGLISH
FOR ACADEMIC PURPOSES

ENGLISH
FOR ACADEMIC PURPOSES

A Handbook for Students

ANDREW GRAHAM

CRITICAL STUDY SKILLS

British Library Cataloguing in Publication Data
A CIP record for this book is available from the British Library
ISBN: 978-1-912508-20-4

This book is also available in the following e-book formats:
MOBI ISBN: 978-1-912508-21-1
EPUB ISBN: 978-1-912508-22-8
Adobe e-book ISBN: 978-1-912508-23-5

Cover design by Out of House Limited
Text design by Out of House Limited
Project Management by Out of House Publishing Solutions
Printed and bound in Great Britain by Bell & Bain, Glasgow

Critical Publishing
3 Connaught Road
St Albans
AL3 5RX

www.criticalpublishing.com

For orders and details of our bulk discounts please go to our website www.criticalpublishing.com or contact our distributor, NBN International,10 Thornbury Road, Plymouth PL6 7PP, telephone 01752 202301 or email orders@nbninternational.com.

Acknowledgements

There has been a tremendous amount of input into this book from both past and present colleagues on the Sino-British Collaborative Programmes at Chengdu University of Technology. In particular, Matt Ryan, Gordon Leonard, Duncan Collis, Mark Hubée, Alex Boyle, Li Zheng, Diane Flick, Richard Smittenaar, Jane Ashley, Maria Enie, David Rhoades, Chen Jiaojiao and Feng Zhiguang (Cody), all of whom have taken the time to provide constructive feedback on ways to improve material used across all units.

Furthermore, students studying on these programmes have also played a crucial role in providing feedback, specifically on how to effectively approach the explanation and practice of each skill. Thanks to their suggestions, this book has been graded to a level that is accessible to non-native English speakers.

Additionally, I would like to say a massive thank you to Simon Aruhan for his continued support and patience. Writing this book was a big challenge, and his efforts to ensure I had the time and necessary comforts to complete this project made the entire process far more manageable.

Finally, I would like to express my sincere appreciation to Tina Richardson for her input throughout this whole project. Her support throughout the draft writing process has been instrumental in the completion of this book. Her suggestions have been extremely constructive and often directed my attention towards areas I would have certainly overlooked without her careful eye.

Andrew Graham
Chengdu University of Technology

Meet the author

Andrew Graham

is an award leader for one of the international foundation programmes (IFPs) at Chengdu University of Technology, China. These programmes have been run in collaboration with UK partner institutions such as Staffordshire, Edge Hill and Oxford Brookes universities. Andrew has worked closely with learners studying English as a second or additional language for over eight years, teaching on a range of modules that centre around research and academic writing, critical thinking, group work and presentation skills. He has contributed to the syllabus design across these modules and created a variety of resources targeted specifically at international students studying for a British qualification.

Contents

Foreword   ix

Introduction   x

Glossary   xii

Unit 01 – Academic writing overview   **1**

1.1 – What is academic writing?   1

1.2 – Features of academic writing   6

Unit 02 – Understanding the topic and planning   **13**

2.1 – Understanding assessment tasks   13

2.2 – Creating new ideas   17

2.3 – Planning an academic paper   19

Unit 03 – Academic arguments   **24**

3.1 – Arguments in writing   24

3.2 – Critical thinking   29

3.3 – Identifying fallacies   31

Unit 04 – Structure: introductions   **38**

4.1 – General statements   38

4.2 – Thesis statements and essay maps   41

Unit 05 – Structure: main body paragraphs   **46**

5.1 – Topic sentences   46

5.2 – Presenting your ideas   50

5.3 – Concluding sentences   55

5.4 – Cohesion   57

Unit 06 – Structure: conclusions   **61**

6.1 – Elements of a conclusion   61

6.2 – Final ideas   64

Unit 07 – Finding evidence   **67**

7.1 – Types of sources   67

7.2 – Types of evidence   70

7.3 – Conducting research   74

7.4 – Reliability   78

Unit 08 – Reading techniques   **89**

8.1 – Reading comprehension   89

8.2 – Skimming and scanning   92

8.3 – SQ3R   94

Unit 09 – Using others' ideas   **97**

9.1 – Preparation   97

9.2 – Paraphrasing   101

9.3 – Summarising   106

9.4 – Translations   109

9.5 – Quotations   112

9.6 – Reporting verbs   115

Unit 10 – Referencing   **119**

10.1 – Understanding referencing   119

10.2 – Citations   123

10.3 – Reference lists   128

Unit 11 – Revision techniques   **136**

11.1 – Feedback   136

11.2 – Improving cohesion   141

11.3 – Proofreading   147

11.4 – Writing checklist   152

Unit 12 – Formatting   **155**

12.1 – Margins, font and spacing   155

12.2 – Cover page and appendices   159

Exercises   **163**

Unit 01 – Academic writing overview   163

Unit 02 – Understanding the topic and planning   167

Unit 03 – Academic arguments   174

Unit 04 – Structure: introductions   176

Unit 05 – Structure: main body paragraphs   183

Unit 06 – Structure: conclusion   190

Unit 07 – Finding evidence   193

Unit 08 – Reading techniques   199

Unit 09 – Using others' ideas   204

Unit 10 – Referencing   212

Unit 11 – Revision techniques   215

Unit 12 – Formatting   218

References   219

Foreword

Andrew Graham has many years' experience of living and working both in the UK and in China. For almost 10 years he has been employed as an English for Academic Purposes (EAP) teacher at a Sino-British institution that is situated in a very large university in Western China. For the last six years he has also had wider course leader and senior management roles within this institution. Andrew's cross-cultural knowledge and experience, together with his years of teaching EAP, provide him with the skills and knowledge to write a significant and key EAP textbook.

What Andrew has achieved in this book has not been by chance or happenstance; rather, it is the result of year-on-year iterations, and use by teachers and students, of institutionally published versions finely tuned into this published edition. The content is based on extensive research – both his own and that of others – and, importantly, from feedback from the students who have used the book. It is research-informed and evidence-based.

Written with up-to-date knowledge of China and, more broadly, Asia, Andrew has used language and has drawn on examples that are in current use and understood by the students who will use the book. Consideration has been given to how each topic should be broken down into sub-topics to aid students' comprehension of how English is used for academic purposes. This step-by-step approach, together with the book's attention to detail, supports students' development in understanding many of the nuances that exist within the English language.

I regard this book as a 'must have' for any international student working towards a British qualification at university. It is also a significant and very useful textbook for English as a Foreign Language (EFL) teachers and students.

Dr Lynn Machin,
PhD/PGCIE Award Leader, Senior Lecturer,
Researcher: Staffordshire University

Introduction

This book contains a collection of material surrounding the skills required by students going into higher education. Specifically, it targets students who are non-native English speakers starting, or about to start, an undergraduate degree. However, it may also be utilised by native English speakers who wish to grasp the necessary skills required to succeed at university. This book has been written in such a way that it could be used as both a course textbook or a self-study guide by students who wish to develop their academic skills.

Terminology and English level

One of the following labels often categorises non-native English students: English as an Additional Language (EAL), English as a Second Language (ESL), or English as a Foreign Language (EFL). There are slight differences between these, such as ESL students only having an understanding of their native language before attempting to learn the English language, while an EAL student may already have a grasp of several other languages beyond their native tongue. Regardless of which category a non-native English student may fall into, this book has been written in a way that should be accessible for students from an intermediate level of English (IELTS 4.0–5.0) and above. The term EAP (English for Academic Purposes) will be used throughout this book to refer to non-native speakers.

Background

The material presented in this book has been gathered over the course of roughly eight years and has taken on many forms within this timeframe. It has extensively been used with students studying for British degrees and diplomas on collaborative programmes in China. Therefore, the content has been adapted in such a way that non-native English speakers can easily grasp the full range of academic skills required to be successful in a variety of undergraduate subjects.

Note to students

To make the most out of this book, you will need to start by reading through each unit in the first half of the book. Each unit will present you with details surrounding vital academic skills. Various steps, examples and tips are presented with each skill, which should aid in your understanding and assist you in completing your academic work.

In the second half of this book, you will find several exercises that will allow you to practise each skill before applying them to your coursework. It is important to refer back to the relevant units while completing each exercise, to ensure that a sensible approach has been taken for each task. Furthermore, when working on assignments for your academic course, it is recommended that you keep this book within reach. This will allow you to improve your understanding of each skill as you approach the wide variety of tasks encountered at university.

Note to teachers

As above, the recommendation is that you work through the units within the first half of this book before moving on to the exercises. Some units are quite detailed and may work better as pre-reading tasks for students to do in their own time. The exercises provided at the back of this book are useful starting points, but the use of supplementary resources is suggested. For a small number of the units, there are no exercises provided as the skills within these sections are covered in more detail in other units.

Although the order of the units has been carefully considered, you may wish to work through this book in an alternative structure. Therefore, each unit begins with a selection of keywords that may not be covered in detail within the unit but may be useful to review at the start of class. Thus, this allows you to jump into any particular section of the book. However, please note that not every new or possibly challenging word has been provided at the start of each unit, as the focus of this vocabulary is on keywords that relate directly to the skills being discussed.

Finally, please be aware that answers to all exercises, as well as some supplementary material, can be accessed via the Critical Publishing website (www.criticalpublishing.com/free-resources).

Glossary

Although each unit does present you with a list of keywords, there is some vocabulary that appears repeatedly throughout the book. Before you go any further, take a few moments to familiarise yourself with the following.

Argument

In writing, argument is the act of researching a topic, gathering ideas from different points of view, and then presenting this information to the reader in support of a claim.

Article

A word used to describe a piece of writing that forms part of a much larger publication (such as a newspaper, magazine, website, or journal).

Assessment/Assignment

In academia, this is a piece of work that is used to evaluate students. It could be a piece of written work, a presentation, or even an exam. Essentially, it is used to measure a student's learning and abilities.

Audience

A name given to the people who will read or watch something. For example, the people who read an essay can be referred to as the audience.

Claim

A statement that strongly presents an idea that you wish to inform the reader about. In academic writing, this is used to present the reader with an argument that will be supported by evidence.

Essay/Paper

These two words are used interchangeably and refer to a piece of writing that students usually complete during education (as an assessment/assignment).

Evidence

A piece of information used to support an idea. This could be a fact, opinion, numbers/data, or reported speech.

Plagiarism

A form of academic cheating that occurs when a student presents the words or ideas of others without telling the reader. This is seen as a serious offence at university and, if found in a piece of work, then action will be taken (usually the work will score zero).

Source

A location where evidence is found. Can be anything from books and journals, to videos and interviews.

Summary

A brief description of a text's most important ideas. Found in conclusions, and many examples of this can be found at the end of each unit in this book.

Unit 01
Academic writing overview

1.1 – What is academic writing?

Keywords

Cohesion	The flow of ideas connecting or uniting as a whole. Achieved through the use of keywords, linking phrases or grammar.
Draft	An early version of an essay. Usually, multiple drafts are created before the final draft (which is submitted for grading).
Objective	Providing ideas that are supported by evidence from different points of view. Not influenced by personal feelings or opinions.

Introduction

Academic writing is often seen as a big challenge for most students starting out at university, and one reason for this can be the fact that many students do not even fully understand what academic writing involves. For international students, the varying styles of writing across the world can further complicate this. Therefore, the best place to start is to briefly introduce the different areas that need to be considered when preparing for and writing an academic paper.

» types of academic papers;

» brainstorming and planning;

» presenting an argument;

» use of sources;

» the writing process.

Types of academic papers

During most university courses there will be a range of assessments. When it comes to written work, there are several types of papers to be aware of.

» **Research essay** – an **objective** paper that will require sufficient evidence to be used throughout in order to support your ideas (ie theories, arguments, etc).

» **Reflective essay** – these are based on personal opinions, thoughts, and feelings. The topic is usually related to a situation you have personally experienced (eg the process and outcome of a group work project).

» **Report** – another objective paper that centres around collected data/statistics. Can be based on external evidence (*secondary research*) or data collected via surveys, questionnaires or interviews (*primary research*).

Unit 01 – Academic writing overview | 1.1 – What is academic writing?

1

» **Literature review** – the name may have you thinking of novels or poetry, but do not let the word *literature* confuse you. These papers include a collection of current research available for a particular topic and are usually done in preparation for an in-depth research essay.

These are just a few examples of papers you will most likely encounter during your time at university, and it is important to identify what is expected for each assignment you receive. The skills covered in this book will focus primarily on research essays, as these are the most commonly encountered papers across most academic courses. However, many of these skills are transferable and can be used in the other types of papers.

Brainstorming and planning

Getting your ideas down on paper and drawing up an outline of your essay's structure before writing any paragraphs is something that you will need to consider. Doing so usually results in a more **cohesive** essay.

Brainstorming

After receiving the details of your assignment, spending some time getting ideas down on paper will help focus your research. It is essential to know what you are searching for before you start looking. The more specific the ideas are, the more refined your search will be, which is especially useful if you rely on the internet for your sources.

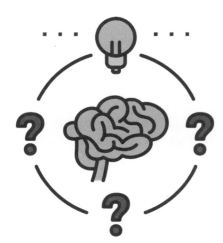

Brainstorming for an academic paper is often done alone, but a broader range of ideas can be gathered by creating a focus group with your peers. It is often helpful to look at a topic from many different points of view, which can be quite challenging to do on your own.

Creating an outline

Planning is an important stage that must be completed before writing begins. The outline forms the foundation of your essay; you can think of it as a blueprint for a building, guiding you in the construction of your ideas.

An outline does not need to be too detailed, as it is likely that some areas will change as your essay is being written. However, the main ideas for each paragraph will likely remain the same, and by deciding their order during the planning stage, your ideas should flow cohesively in the final essay.

Do not forget to keep your outline close by as you write your essay. Try referring back to your outline after each paragraph has been written, just to check you have covered every point, and so that you know what the next paragraph is going to focus on before you carry on writing.

Presenting an argument

In academic writing, it is important to present a range of ideas that collectively form an argument. This does not mean you are trying to fight with the reader. In fact, the purpose is to present a position that can be defended through the use of evidence.

Argument versus persuasion

It is important to understand the difference between argument and persuasion, as many students often interpret these two styles of writing as being the same. Below is a table, adapted from Read Write Think (no date), outlining the different approaches taken when writing a research paper in each style.

Argumentative style	Persuasive style
Choose your topic, do some research, **then** decide which side you are going to support with your argument	Choose your topic, **then** decide which side you are going to support
Use your essay to **show the reader** why you have chosen to support this side	Use your essay to **get the reader to agree** with your chosen side
Offer the reader an **objective selection of evidence** that shows your ideas are valid	Use **evidence with your own personal emotion and/or opinions** to convince the reader that your ideas are correct
Recognise and **present counter-arguments**	Ignore and **avoid counter-arguments**
Provide **evidence with every idea**	Provide **some ideas without evidence**
Write in a **calm tone**, with the aim to **inform the reader** of your choice	Write in an **emotional tone, aggressively trying to change the reader's opinion**

As you may have guessed, the argumentative style is balanced and more appropriate in academic writing. Therefore, throughout this book, the focus will be on planning and writing in an argumentative style.

Use of sources

To be objective in your own writing, you will need to make use of evidence to support your ideas. This will require you to do some research surrounding your topic. At first, research is used to gain knowledge and form ideas during the brainstorming and planning stages. However, you cannot simply gather ideas from the sources and present them as your own. You will need to present the sources in your paper to demonstrate their relationship to the point you are trying to make.

Research is an ongoing process that continues throughout the writing process, from the early stages of planning, all the way until you begin to revise and proofread the final draft of your essay. As new information is constantly being published (especially online), it is essential for you to keep looking for articles relating to your topic.

Paraphrasing and summarising

When using evidence in your papers, you should avoid copying the exact words of the original author. Although it is sometimes acceptable to directly 'quote' a source (especially for extracts from interviews), the more accepted approach is to use paraphrasing and/or summarising.

Both of these methods allow you to present the ideas of others using your own words, which is an important skill to master in academic writing.

Referencing

Whenever evidence is used in your papers, whether it is an idea (in the form of a paraphrase or summary) or a direct 'quotation', you need to provide information telling the reader where to find the original source.

You have to be transparent and honest with the reader that this information is not your own. Furthermore, your essay is unlikely to cover every detail contained in the original source. Therefore, providing a reference allows the reader to go and learn more about the ideas you have mentioned in your work.

The writing process

Some of the stages in the writing process have already been mentioned above, but there are a few more areas you need to consider when writing an academic paper. Below is an outline of a typical writing process that many students follow when writing an academic paper.

Understanding the topic

In most assignments at university, your tutor will provide you with a topic in the form of an assessment task. All the information needed to start brainstorming, planning and researching the topic will be found here.

Sometimes the topic may be quite broad, and you will be expected to narrow this down into a more focused area. If this is the case, once you have brainstormed ideas and conducted some basic research, your final topic should be checked by your tutor before you begin writing.

Draft writing

Everyone makes mistakes, and you can use these as a learning opportunity. This is why it is necessary to go through a draft writing process. The first draft will give you and your tutor a clearer idea of what areas need extra attention. If you only ever write one draft before a deadline, do not expect to get a good grade.

Draft writing is a step-by-step process, so do not rush to fix everything in one go. Leave smaller problems until later, such as spelling and tidying up grammar, which can wait until the proofreading stage.

For the first few revisions of your essay, focus on your ideas, the evidence you are using, and overall essay cohesion. Remember to pay close attention to the details your tutor gave you in the assessment task.

Each draft will be an improvement over the last, but there will still be areas that can be improved. The draft writing process is reflective and requires you to look at what you have done and identify ways to improve. The more drafts you attempt, the stronger your essay will become. However, remember you are not just writing and rewriting; you should primarily be looking for problems in your essay and finding ways to fix these issues.

Proofreading

This should be the final stage of revision before submitting your final draft. This is the time to focus your attention towards spelling, grammar and punctuation errors. However, this is also a perfect opportunity to improve your vocabulary use by changing repetitive words or replacing simple vocabulary with academic alternatives. Furthermore, if the formatting of your essay is also going to be graded, this is also the right time to check for any issues regarding font sizes, typeface choices, line spacing and margins.

Finally, although you should keep your reference list updated as you write, this is also an ideal time to make sure all your references are present and correctly formatted according to the reference style of your university.

Summary ✔

Although this unit has only presented you with a brief introduction to academic writing and the areas that need to be considered, you should now have a clearer idea of what to expect throughout the rest of this book. There will be other skills required to create a robust academic paper, but the most important aspects have been highlighted here, and there should be no significant surprises as you progress through the following units.

References

Read Write Think (no date) *What is the Difference between Persuasive and Argumentative Writing?* Available at: www.readwritethink.org/files/resources/lesson-docs/Difference_Between_Persuasive_Argumentative.pdf (Accessed: 9 June 2018).

1.2 – Features of academic writing

Keywords

Brainstorm	The act of gathering and creating ideas.
Citation	Provided whenever evidence has been used in an essay. Part of the referencing process.
Concluding sentence	Used to signal that the current idea has been explored in sufficient detail.
Draft	An early version of an essay. Usually, multiple drafts are created before the final draft (which is submitted for grading).
Inductive reasoning	An approach used when forming arguments. The method of taking specific examples and creating a generalised claim.
Reference list	Given at the end of an essay. Provides further details that are not given alongside the citation (eg book title, website URL).
Thesis statement	A sentence provided in the introduction paragraph. This will outline the main claim of the entire essay.
Topic sentence	A sentence given at the start of each main body paragraph to express the main idea that will be explored within.

Introduction

When writing an academic paper, you will need to consider the language used, how paragraphs and sentences are structured, and the way you convey your ideas. In this unit, you will encounter six common features of academic writing that must be used in your papers. However, you will find that for some essay topics (eg personal reflections) you will not need to apply all six features. Therefore, try not to think of them as rigid rules that you must always follow, but guidelines that help shape your writing into an academic form.

1. Complexity

The way English is spoken is entirely different from the way it is written. Spoken language is usually flexible, and the correct meaning can easily be conveyed even when there are grammatical errors or poor vocabulary choices. When speaking, if your audience does not fully understand your meaning, they can ask you questions.

However, you are not usually present when a reader is looking at your written work. Therefore, you need to make sure that both grammar and vocabulary are clear and accurate. Furthermore, you will often be asked to write an essay within a specific word limit. This requires you to be concise with your language, avoiding long and wordy sentences.

In the following examples, you should be able to see clear differences in both length and vocabulary choices.

> ### * Example – spoken text
>
> *Cities in Britain are no longer considered to be as safe as they once were, as there are now many crimes taking place on a regular basis.*

> ### * Example – written text
>
> *Crime rates have now risen across Britain's once peaceful cities.*

Lexical items

Lexical items are single words, a chain of words, or phrases that are the basic building blocks of language. Essentially, independently these items can carry a specific meaning, whereas grammatical words (eg conjunctions, particles, determiners) are either ambiguous or hold very little meaning when presented alone. Try to present a higher ratio of lexical items within your writing.

Nominalisations

Shifting the focus of sentences away from the actions (verbs) onto an object or concept (nouns) is standard practice within academic writing. By doing this, your writing not only becomes more complex but also aids in developing some of the other features covered by this unit (such as formality and objectivity).

Noun phrases

A grouping of words that contain a noun and a modifier. These are used in sentences as subjects, things, or prepositional objects (just like a common noun). Noun phrases are an excellent alternative for both the overuse of verbs and 'wh-' clauses (ie subordinate clauses that are introduced by what, who, which, when, where, why, and how).

Lexical variation

If a piece of writing repeats certain words and phrases throughout, the reader may feel the article is too simple. Therefore, it is essential to present the reader with a wide-ranging and varied vocabulary. Both nominalisations and noun phrases will aid in adding variety to your writing.

2. Formality

In many ways, this is quite similar to complexity. However, this feature is focused towards vocabulary choice and writing style. Below are a few examples of what you should avoid in your academic papers.

Colloquial words and expressions

These are words that are often heard in spoken English. The problem is that these words can often sound quite simple or vague in meaning. You should especially avoid language that is frequently used in social media and messaging apps.

> ### * Example
>
> *stuff / things / sort of / yeah / nice / gonna / cool*

Contracted forms

Although these may sound natural in spoken language, they can appear rather informal within an academic text. However, you may notice while reading academic papers (such as journals) that they are sometimes used, but when they are, they are used sparingly. Therefore, it is always safer to simply avoid their use.

> ### * Example
>
> *can't / don't / couldn't / doesn't / shouldn't / hasn't*

Two-word verbs (phrasal verbs)

Attempting to write an academic essay without using any phrasal verbs is almost impossible. There are times when they are necessary, but they should be kept to an absolute minimum. For the large majority of phrasal verbs, you will be able to find a suitable replacement.

> *call off / carry on / boot up / add up / find out / turn down*

Vague statements

In almost all cases of academic writing, you are required to be as precise as possible. This means providing the reader with as many details as possible. This is especially true when dealing with numbers. The only exception to this is when interpreting data from a visual source such as a chart or graph.

> *a lot of / etc / and so on / everybody knows / as is known to all*

Asking (rhetorical) questions

There is no specific reason why these should be avoided, but they are often seen to be annoying for the reader to encounter while working their way through an essay. Your reader does not want to be presented with questions that you will answer in the next few sentences; they simply want you to get on with exploring the topic. Furthermore, asking and answering questions conveys a conversational structure, which then breaks the formality and is perceived as a casual conversation.

> *"What should be done in this situation? Well, maybe the first step is to…"*

3. Objectivity

To be objective, you need to make sure that you do not provide personal thoughts or opinions while writing your essay (unless it is a reflective topic related to your own personal experience). You need to pay particular attention to your use of pronouns.

Avoid first-person pronouns

The reader wants you to share what you have discovered while researching your topic. Unless you are a professional, or a respected figure in your field of study, your reader will not want to hear what you 'think' or 'believe'. You will need to provide evidence that you have collected from a range of sources, and only then will the reader be interested in the information you have presented in support of your essay's argument.

> *I / me / myself / we / our / ourselves / I think… / In my opinion / I believe…*

Avoid second-person pronouns

Talking directly to the reader is another form of writing that should be avoided in your academic essays, as this can be misleading and unnecessary. Your reader may not be associated with the topic you are exploring, and therefore may feel your directions are irrelevant.

> *you / your / yourself / you should… / you can… / it is up to you…*

4. Explicitness

Being explicit in your writing primarily relates to two areas: being clear about the relationship between ideas, and stating where you sourced your evidence.

Cohesion

You should clearly demonstrate how ideas are connected throughout your entire essay. This is done by using cohesive devices such as a **thesis statement**, **topic sentences**, and **concluding sentences**. All of these are used to tie paragraphs together through common themes, such as the overall argument of an essay.

However, it is also important to use cohesion within paragraphs to link from one sentence to the next. To achieve this, you are encouraged to use discourse markers. Below is a table containing some discourse markers that may be useful for improving cohesion between sentences.

Explicit use	Discourse marker	Explicit use	Discourse marker
Giving more information	*In addition...* *Additionally...* *Moreover...* *Furthermore...*	**Emphasising**	*In particular...* *Especially...* *Above all...* *Significantly...*
Giving examples	*For example...* *For instance...* *Namely...* *Such as...*	**Cause and effect**	*Therefore...* *Consequently...* *Thus...* *Hence...*
Summarising	*In summary...* *In conclusion...* *In short...* *In brief...*	**Contrasting ideas**	*However...* *Whereas...* *Alternatively...* *Conversely...*
Sequencing ideas	*First...* *Second...* *Finally...* *The former...* *The latter...* *Meanwhile...* *Subsequently...*	**Comparing ideas**	*Similarly...* *Likewise...* *Equally...* *In the same way...*

Referencing

When words or ideas from your research have been used in your essay, you will need to inform the reader of where this information was originally located. It does not matter what type of source you have used (books, websites, journals, videos, or even a lecture you attended), you will need to provide the reader with details of when these have been used in your essay's paragraphs (in the form of **citations**). Furthermore, for every citation you provide, you will also need to create an entry in the **reference list** at the end of your essay.

5. Hedging

Academic writing, especially argumentative writing, is based on facts and evidence. However, the strength of the evidence you use and/or the idea that is being supported may have some weaknesses. The connections being made may make sense, but there may not be a direct correlation, and this is where hedging is essential.

Also known as cautious language, hedging is used to express what level of certainty you have regarding the claim you are making. You will need to decide how strongly you support the idea before writing it down in your essay. This decision will then dictate what level of hedging will be required when presenting your claims.

In most cases, when working with statistics, data and facts, hedging will usually be unnecessary. However, when presenting a claim provided by another author, you will need to carefully decide how well they have supported their ideas before providing them in your essay. Additionally, hedging plays an important role in the presentation of arguments that were formed through the use of **inductive reasoning**. Below are some examples of vocabulary used in hedging.

Grammatical form	Example
Introductory verbs	*seem / tend / looks like / appear to be / think / believe / doubt / be sure / indicate / suggest*
Lexical verbs	*believe / assume / suggest*
Modal verbs	*will / must / would / may / might / could*
Adverbs of frequency	*often / sometimes / usually*
Modal adverbs	*certainly / definitely / clearly / probably / possibly / perhaps / conceivably*
Modal adjectives	*certain / definite / clear / probable / possible*
Modal nouns	*assumption / possibility / probability*
That clauses	*It could be that... / It might be suggested that...*
To-clauses + adjective	*It may be possible to obtain... / It is useful to study... / It is important to develop...*

6. Planning

When you are tasked with writing an academic paper, you will need to think very carefully about how to divide up your time. You will first need to understand the assessment task, **brainstorm** some ideas, gather research and then draw up an outline that you plan to follow.

Planning does not only include details of what information will be included in the final paper; you will need to consider how to manage your time. It is important to go through a **draft** writing process, which means planning when each version needs to be completed by and allowing time for feedback opportunities with your tutor.

Summary ✔

It is important to remember that this unit has only introduced some key features of academic writing, and that these are not to be treated as rigid rules that must always be followed. As you read papers written by others, you will notice more patterns and features that are commonly used in academic writing.

Some of the features mentioned in this unit will appear elsewhere in this book, but some of them (especially surrounding grammatical rules) will not be covered in great detail. If you are struggling to grasp the way in which specific grammatical rules are applied, then you should definitely check out *Practical English Usage by Michal Swan* (details can be found below).

Further reading

For more details about the features of academic writing and grammatical rules mentioned in this unit, check out the following resources:

Gillett, A. Hammond, A. and Martala, M. (2009) *Inside Track to Successful Academic Writing*. Harlow, Essex: Pearson Education Limited.

Swan, M. (2016) *Practical English Usage*. 4th edn. Oxford: Oxford University Press.

Unit 02
Understanding the topic and planning

2.1 – Understanding assessment tasks

Keywords

Assignment brief	A document outlining details such as: the assessment task, deadlines, and how the work will be graded.
Deadline	The date and time when your final version must be submitted for grading.
Draft	An early version of an essay. Usually, multiple drafts are created before the final draft (which is submitted for grading).
Learning outcome	A statement that describes the knowledge or skill that should be gained through a module or assessment.
Marking criteria	Details how an assignment is divided up (usually represented as a percentage).
Marking rubric	Primarily used by teachers to grade assessments. These provide the targets for each criteria and define the difference between pass and fail (and other grade boundaries).

Introduction

The sooner you have a good understanding of what you need to do, the easier the rest of the writing process will be. Before you begin planning out your essay, you need to make sure that you have read all instructions carefully. Your tutors should provide you with an **assignment brief** that includes the following details.

» assignment title;

» **deadline** and submission details;

» **learning outcomes** of the assignment;

» assessment task(s);

» rules and regulations (such as word limits);

» **marking criteria** and **rubric**.

Breaking down the assessment task

In the assignment brief, the assessment task is often provided as a complex set of sentences that may not always provide the clearest of instructions. Sometimes your tutor may highlight a particular question to focus on, but often the aim/topic of the assignment has to be independently uncovered.

When you are first given an assessment task, follow these steps.

» Read the assessment several times to make sure you are not missing anything.

» Underline or highlight the 'task' words.

» Underline words that give details about the subject or wider topic.

» Identify how many sections there are in the task (are you required to answer multiple questions or cover several different aspects?).

Be prepared to spend a long time reviewing the assessment task. Following the steps above should provide you with a clearer idea of what is expected. However, do not be afraid to contact your tutor if you are still unsure. Starting the task incorrectly will waste both your time and the tutor's time.

Task words

Assignment briefs will provide you with at least one, but often more, of the following task words.

» **Analyse** – review (something) in detail to discover its meaning, the steps/stages of its processes, and highlight the most important points/features.

» **Discuss** – write about the most important aspects, provide arguments for and against, and consider what the outcome may be.

» **Evaluate** – consider the advantages and disadvantages, review the strength of evidence on both sides. Use these details to reach an informed decision.

» **Examine** – take a close look at a subject to discover the way it works and what conditions are required for it to function.

» **Explain** – provide a clear description as to what something is, why something happened the way it did, or why things are done in a specific way.

» **Illustrate** – through the use of evidence/examples, present a clear picture in your reader's mind about a particular subject.

» **Justify** – give evidence that supports an argument or idea. Explain why a decision or conclusion has been made for this side of the argument.

» **Suggest** – consider a situation and provide suggestions for changes/improvements. Must be carefully backed up by evidence in support of how this action could help.

Subject/focus words

The assessment task will also contain several words that are there to narrow the topic down to a specific area of focus. For example, you may be writing a paper related to marketing, but you may be asked to write about marketing methods used in the hospitality industry. Therefore, you may find words such as 'hotels', 'restaurants', and 'catering'. These words are given to focus your attention, while also limiting your research field and the amount you can write about. Sometimes these words are overlooked, and this can lead to a broad and overly descriptive paper.

Marking rubrics

If you are still confused by the assessment task, then another place to look is the marking rubric. Your tutors will refer to this when they are grading your final submission, and therefore it contains a lot of details about what should be included in your paper.

The marking rubric should be given to you at the same time as the assessment task (it is usually part of the assignment brief). However, if this is not provided to you, then you should certainly contact your tutor and ask for a copy.

Marking rubrics come in many forms, but they are often broken up by criteria and grading boundaries. The way they are structured can vary between different universities, and even between different departments/courses within a university. Below is an example of what a typical marking rubric may look like.

Criteria: Topic (30%)

Distinction (70–100%)	Merit (60–69%)	Pass (40–59%)	Fail (0–39%)
Has provided an answer to all three questions.	Has answered two out of three questions.	Has only answered one of the questions in sufficient detail.	Has not sufficiently answered any of the questions provided.
Every answer is supported by at least two sources.	Every answer is supported by at least one source.	Has provided support, but from a questionable source.	Has not used any reliable sources to support answers.
Has provided counter-arguments for every claim.	Has provided at least one counter-argument.	Highlights a possible counter-argument but does not explore in detail.	Does not mention any counter-arguments.

The marking rubric should constantly be reviewed throughout the writing process. Every time you complete a **draft** of your paper, review the marking rubric and see where you think your paper is currently landing in the rubric. Identify areas where you can gain extra marks and work those changes into your next draft.

Summary ✔

At university, you are expected to be more independent and are often required to figure out many things on your own. However, your tutors are not trying to trick you or set you up for failure. When they are writing the assessment tasks, they may feel that everything is clear and present in the assignment brief – but you may see things differently. If you are at all unsure, then approach your tutor and tell them what you think it is you need to do. They will either confirm you are correct, or they will point you in the right direction.

Sometimes it is worth spending a little more time thinking about the task before you even begin to do any planning. Creating ideas for your essay and writing down a plan will be worthless if they are not on task. Returning to and reviewing the assignment brief is recommended, as sometimes even if you start well, you may begin to stray off course.

2.2 – Creating new ideas

Keywords

Creativity	The act of generating or recognising new ideas, usually with the aim of solving problems.
Linear notes	Notes that are structured in the order that information is received, often used when taking notes during a lecture.
Mind map	A diagram that is used to visually present ideas. The centre of the image focuses on the main idea, with related ideas branching outwards.

Introduction

Writing an academic paper requires an element of **creativity**, as you are often asked to present new and interesting ideas, or at least gather information from various sources and use these details to support an idea from a different point of view. This means you will need to understand your topic carefully and gather as many ideas about a subject as possible, before picking out the best ideas to create an outline of your essay.

Brainstorming

Once you have understood the assessment task, the next stage is to come up with ideas that relate to the subject/topic that will aid in supporting the purpose of your paper (eg to *examine*, *analyse*, or *discuss*). Usually, this is done before any research is conducted. However, if you are unfamiliar with the topic, it may be a good idea to do a little background reading first.

Brainstorming is essentially a tool used to get your ideas down on paper. This can be a very straightforward note-taking activity, or if you are a more visual individual, it can be a very colourful and creative process. The way in which you create a brainstorm really depends on your personality. But, it may also depend on how much time you have available.

Linear notes (example)

Brainstorm - Essay writing

Introduction	Main body	Conclusion
- Opening sentence (hook)	- Topic sentence	- Restate claim
- General statements	- Supporting point	- Summary
- Background info.	- Evidence / example	- Final idea
- Thesis statement	- Discussion	- Suggestion
- Essay map	- Concluding sentence	- Prediction

Mind map (example)

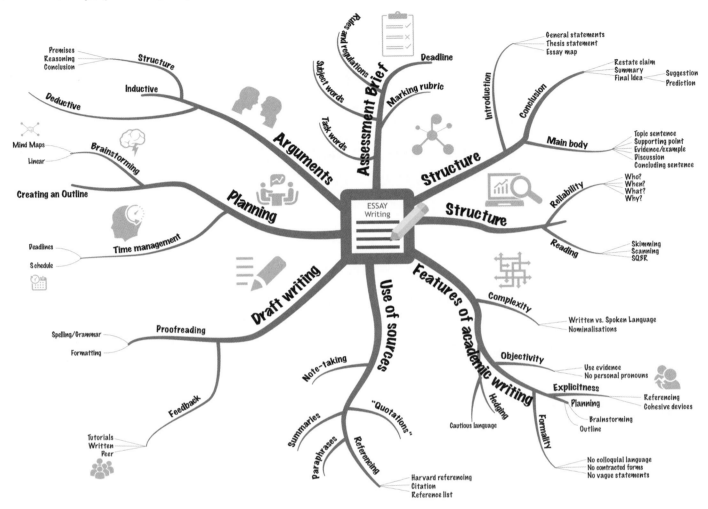

The power of group thinking

The process of brainstorming is usually done alone, but it can also be done in groups. If you get the chance to work with others during this stage, you will be able to collect a broader range of ideas than you would usually be able to when doing this alone. However, the more ideas you collect, the risk of you straying off topic becomes more probable. Be concise, and make sure you only take forward the most relevant and useful ideas for covering your topic sufficiently.

Summary ✔

This unit has presented you with two examples of how to record your brainstorming, but do not limit yourself. This is a very personal process, and it is up to you to decide which way works best for you. The main point is to get as many useful ideas as possible down on paper, which will then aid in the planning of your essay.

2.3 – Planning an academic paper

Keywords

Assignment brief A document outlining details such as the assessment task, deadlines, and how the work will be graded.

Time management The ability to control and effectively plan how your time is divided.

Introduction

Planning your paper is more than just writing a list of ideas that you wish to include. First, you should set yourself goals, or more specifically, deadlines. Your tutor will provide you with a final deadline, but you should think about the steps you will need to take in the writing process. Once you have a schedule, you can then take your ideas and create an outline. This is when you start to think about the structure and in which section of the essay you will use your ideas.

Time management

As mentioned above, your tutor will provide you with a final deadline, which is usually stated in the **assignment brief**. From this deadline, you should work backwards and give yourself enough time to write the essay. It is essential to allow yourself enough time to plan, research, write, and check your work.

Therefore, you will need to pull out your calendar and make a note of your final deadline. Then, create a schedule by setting yourself some smaller goals between now and submission date. Here is an example of how your time may be divided up for an essay that has to be written over a four-week period.

Week 01 – Planning

» **Day 01** – receive the assignment brief, review the assessment task and begin brainstorming.

» **Day 03** – begin working on an outline and start conducting research.

» **Day 06** – finish the outline, continue to do research, and begin writing the first draft.

Week 02 – Writing the first draft

» **Day 13** – first draft is finished, continue with research, arrange a tutorial or email draft to tutor for review.

Week 03 – Reviewing feedback and writing the second draft

» **Day 15** – meet with tutor (or receive email from tutor with comments). Review feedback and make decisions on how to make changes. Research continues while working on the second draft.

Week 04 – Final review, proofreading and submission

» **Day 22** – second draft is finished, essay is reviewed and checked against the marking rubric. Consider what changes can be made to achieve the desired score. No major changes should be made after this stage.

» **Day 26** – a third draft is finished, and research is completed. The essay is now proofread for language and formatting errors.

» **Day 28** – the final version is ready to be submitted and should be turned in well before the deadline (to avoid any possible technical issues encountered while submitting).

Structuring a research essay

When writing a research-based essay, there are three main sections used to form the overall structure of the paper. These sections will be covered in more detail elsewhere in this book, but in the following you will find a brief introduction to how each of these sections are formed.

Introduction

The introduction gives the reader background information, and sets up the main claim of the entire essay.

» Provide some information about the broader topic and get the reader familiar with the subject.

» Present the essay's main claim. This is provided as a statement, followed by a brief summary of the essay's main ideas.

Main body paragraphs

This section contains many paragraphs, each one focusing on a specific idea that supports the main claim provided in the introduction.

» Each paragraph starts with a sentence informing the reader of the idea that will be covered within.

» The rest of the paragraph then follows a three-step process that may be repeated as many times as needed until enough detail has been provided in support of the essay's claim.

» The three-step process includes 1) a supporting point, 2) evidence or an example that supports this point, and 3) a discussion that shows the link between what the evidence states, the supporting point, and the claim made during the introduction.

» Finally, the paragraph is wrapped up using a concluding sentence. This informs the reader that the current idea has been fully explored, while also offering a hint or connection to the following body paragraph.

English for Academic Purposes: A Handbook for Students

Conclusion

The final paragraph of the essay, which provides the reader with a review of the main ideas covered in the previous paragraphs and provides closure to the topic.

» The essay's main claim should be restated, reminding the reader why this paper was written (what was the aim/purpose of the essay).

» Present a summary of the main (and most interesting) ideas to help remind the reader of what information has been provided in support of the main claim.

» Finally, finish off with an interesting idea. This is the last chance to impress the reader and should be something that leaves them thinking about the essay even after they have finished reading it.

Paragraphs and word counts

Students will often ask: *'How many paragraphs should I write?'* Unfortunately, there is no definitive answer to this question. It depends on many factors, such as the topic, the type of argument, the word limit, or how you plan to present your ideas.

A recommended method for working this out is to brainstorm your ideas first, then consider your word limit. If you are asked to write an essay of 1,500 words, and you have gathered at least four strong ideas, you could break your paper down as follows.

Paragraph	Word count
Introduction	*150 words*
Paragraph 1 (idea 1)	*300 words*
Paragraph 2 (idea 2)	*300 words*
Paragraph 3 (idea 3)	*300 words*
Paragraph 4 (idea 4)	*300 words*
Conclusion	*150 words*
TOTAL:	1,500 words

The introduction and conclusion are often recommended to be roughly 10 per cent of your word limit (each). For the main body paragraphs, you should keep them as balanced as possible. Therefore, they should be roughly the same word count (as above). If you think you can sufficiently cover each idea in 300 words, then this six-paragraph structure should work.

However, if you feel one of your ideas is a little weaker than the others, then you may need to devote higher word counts to the other three ideas and remove the weaker one from the essay entirely.

Additionally, another benefit of looking at your essay in this way is to ease the panic that some students feel when they are asked to write an assignment with a high word limit. By breaking it down into smaller chunks, the overall task becomes more manageable and less intimidating.

Creating an outline

An outline is a visual representation of your essay, which you could consider as a map, or even a blueprint for a building. This is useful for guiding your research and the general writing of your paper. It does not need to include a lot of detail; it should simply state what ideas you plan to focus on, where you will place these within the essay, and how you plan to present them.

The truth is, the final draft of your essay and the outline will probably be different. Even your first draft may have minor differences based on what you discover during your research. This is normal, and you should not worry if things change over the course of the writing process.

However, do not think that making a plan is pointless just because changes are likely to happen. By taking the time to write a plan in the first place, you have given yourself some direction and focused your attention towards the areas where research and writing can begin. Students that go through the planning stage usually always produce a stronger paper compared to those who just start writing straight away.

Outline (example)

Introduction

Thesis: the structure of an academic essay needs to be carefully considered in order to be cohesive.

*Reminder: need to find evidence for supporting points

Main body paragraph 1

Topic sentence: introductions should provide background and direction.

Supporting point 1: general statements guide readers into the subject.

Supporting point 2: thesis statements sets the theme for the entire essay.

Main body paragraph 2

Topic sentence: main body paragraphs should smoothly flow between ideas.

Supporting point 1: topic sentences provide a controlling idea for paragraph.

Supporting point 2: using repeated steps for points = easier understanding.

Main body paragraph 3

Topic sentence: a concluding paragraph helps tie everything together.

Supporting point 1: thesis is restated to remind the remind the reader.

Supporting point 2: summaries the main points to leave deep impression.

English for Academic Purposes: A Handbook for Students

Details of your conclusion are not always necessary during the creation of an outline, as the information you will include here may be difficult to predict during the planning stage. You may have a particular argument you want to prove, but until you conduct your research and discover the truth, the conclusion is virtually unknown.

The outline should be adapted and added to as you conduct your research. Make notes about what evidence you will use for each point, the source details (eg authors, book names, and website URLs), and any particular experts that are well known for writing about your particular topic. Basically, write down anything you feel will aid in the process of writing your essay.

Summary ✔

When it comes to planning your essay, you do not only have to think about what will be included in your paper; you also need to think carefully about time management. Knowing what needs to be done and when it needs to be done by will ensure that each section has been sufficiently considered. One of the biggest reasons for failing an assignment is leaving everything until the last minute and rushing to complete the paper in the days leading up to the final deadline.

Creating an outline is a great way to form a strong foundation. However, do not limit yourself, and remember to make suitable changes as you conduct your research and begin writing your actual paper. Refer back to your outline, and keep updating it as you go, as this provides you with a visual representation of your essay you can refer to when checking your drafts at a later stage.

Unit 03
Academic arguments

3.1 – Arguments in writing

Keywords

Counter-argument	An idea or conclusion that is the opposite of the claim being made in what you are defending.
Deductive reasoning	An approach used when forming arguments. The claim is decided first; then research is conducted to confirm if the claim is true or false.
Hedging	Cautious language that is used when presenting ideas that have some level of doubt regarding the validity or certainty.
Inductive reasoning	An approach used when forming arguments. The method of taking specific examples and creating a generalised claim.
Rebuttal	A statement given to disprove an idea. Used to disprove or highlight weaknesses in a counter-argument.
Sound	A way to describe something as strong. A sound argument would be considered as true and logical.
Unsound	A way to describe something as weak. An unsound argument would be considered as untrue and illogical.

Introduction

In academia, arguments are considered to be a form of debate. You may think of a debate as a group of people sitting around a table providing emotional statements in support of their claims. However, academic debates are based on reason and should be as far removed from emotion as possible. Therefore, in academic writing, whenever you present a claim that you wish to prove, it needs to be backed up with evidential support and logical reasoning.

Elements of an argument

When presenting an argument, there are certain elements that are provided together to give the reader a logical and well-supported argument. It is important to note that at this stage, you will be presented with a breakdown of how an argument is formed. However, when you reach the unit on essay structure, specifically main body paragraphs, the terminology used will be simplified to help you understand how an argument can be presented in your essays.

Premise(s)

As mentioned in the introduction, an argument needs to be backed up by evidence. This should be a range of facts or ideas presented by others that will support the claim you are trying to prove. This part of an argument is referred to as the premise. Without this, you cannot successfully argue your point.

Conclusion

Your conclusion (in an argument) is based on the evidence that you have discovered. By reading the evidence, you should have formed your own idea that you wish to provide in your essay. Essentially, this is your 'claim'; the idea you wish to debate.

Reasoning

Although you may think your idea is clear, especially when you have provided the evidence alongside it, you still need to show the connection between what you are claiming and how you reached this idea. You will have spent a long time planning, researching and writing your essay, which means it all seems logical and easy to understand. However, the reasoning element of an argument is important for your reader, as they may not have a deep understanding of the topic.

Deductive and inductive reasoning

There are two main approaches to how an argument is formed, and this depends on what element of the argument you are starting with. In science-based subjects, deductive arguments are usually required throughout. In social-based subjects, you may provide a mixture of both deductive and inductive arguments. However, inductive arguments can be more open-ended and will need to be carefully presented through the use of **hedging**.

Deductive reasoning

This type of reasoning is sometimes informally referred to as the 'top-down' approach. When forming a deductive argument, you will begin with an idea that you are trying to prove. From here, you will then conduct research or experiments to try and prove if this argument is true (*valid*) or not (*invalid*). In the following are some examples of deductive reasoning, and the different outcomes.

---

* Example – valid and sound

Mark is taller than Tom, and Harry is shorter than Tom. Therefore, Mark is taller than Harry.

In this argument, the reasoning is **sound**. The premises provided support the final (and valid) conclusion. This is a basic, but strong, example of deductive reasoning.

Sometimes when constructing an argument, one or more elements may be misinterpreted or incorrectly used. This then leads to some examples of weak (**unsound**) arguments.

---

* Example – invalid, but with true premise(s)

All snakes are cold-blooded. All snails are cold-blooded. Therefore, all snakes are snails.

The premises that state that both snakes and snails are cold-blooded are true, but the conclusion that has been reached is untrue.

* Example – valid, but with untrue premise(s)

All cats can fly. Felix is a cat. Therefore, Felix can fly.

Although the conclusion is valid, not every premise is true. This means that the entire claim is unsound.

Inductive reasoning

This type of argument is considered to be the opposite of deductive reasoning and is informally referred to as the 'bottom-up' approach. This time, the argument is formed by gathering specific evidence or examples and then creating a broad conclusion based on this information. Basically, the conclusion is created based on any patterns discovered in a range of similar situations. This is why hedging is required when presenting a claim based on inductive reasoning, because although the conclusion seems logical, it may not always be true in every situation.

The level of traffic always increases outside the university after 5pm. Therefore, it is likely that traffic outside every university in the city increases after 5pm.

Here you can see there is an observation of increased traffic occurring regularly outside one university. This has led to the conclusion that this same situation may be found outside every university in the city. The premise does support the conclusion, as this may be true, but it is not strong enough to be seen as a sound and logical argument.

The inclusion of the phrase *'it is likely that'* does provide a level of hedging. This would inform the reader that this conclusion is not being presented as a strong argument, but an idea that may go towards supporting a much larger claim (perhaps the overall claim within the essay).

Argumentative versus persuasive writing

For an argumentative essay to be successful, it should remain objective throughout. On the contrary, in persuasive writing you will often include emotion and attempts at changing the opinion of your reader. This is not the purpose of an argumentative essay, as the ideas should be sufficiently supported by evidence. This will allow the reader to make their own informed decision based on how successfully you have presented your claims.

Some differences between these two styles of writing were introduced in Unit 01, but below is a summary of what you should be paying attention to when writing in an argumentative style.

» The side of the argument you have chosen to support is decided based on some preliminary research.

» The aim is to inform the reader about the topic while providing a range of objective evidence that further supports the reasoning behind your choice.

» Take the time to present the opposite opinions (via **counter-arguments**). Provide evidence for every idea, on both sides of the argument.

» Remain calm and use formal language to educate the reader on the topic. Avoid the use of any personal or emotional language.

Presenting counter-arguments

During the researching stage, be sure to look into both sides of any arguments surrounding your topic. You should have made a decision to support one side over the other, but you need to at least understand why there is an opposing view. This will ensure your paper is objective, as you have demonstrated an understanding of different sides in an argument, and you haven't tried to hide this from the reader.

You will need to present your own claim first and provide a strong set of premises that support this conclusion. Only then can you present the counter-argument, which will also need support from some form of evidence. Here is an outline of how to objectively present an argument:

» your claim (*conclusion*);

» evidence to support your claim (*premise*);

» discussion to support your claim (*reasoning*);

» a claim that opposes your own (*counter-argument*);

» a discussion to refute this opposing claim (**rebuttal**).

Counter-argument

The counter-argument should be presented in a similar way to your own claim. However, it should be introduced through the use of a cohesive device that highlights that the following claim is an opposing view. You could use **discourse markers** (eg 'However' and 'Alternatively'), or a phrase that demonstrates opposition (eg 'The opposing view is', or 'Another view is that').

Rebuttal

At this stage, you will need to provide a discussion that highlights weaknesses in the counter-argument. Furthermore, you should refer back to the strengths of your original claim. It is critical that both your original claim and the counter-argument are somewhat related. This is because if your counter-argument is very different from your original claim, your rebuttal will be unsuccessful.

One way to find weaknesses in a counter-argument is to identify when invalid reasoning has been used. For example, you may have found a statement that concludes with a valid claim, but some of the premises used to reach this conclusion are untrue. Your rebuttal would then identify the untrue premises and confirm why your original claim is a sound alternative.

Summary ✔

Constructing and presenting an argument successfully takes a lot of careful planning and research. You will need to take the time to read around the subject and be sure to collect details from all sides of the argument before presenting your claims.

The type of reasoning used when forming your arguments will need to be made obvious to your readers, as your audience may be a mix of experts and the uninformed. This means that if you try to present a claim formed through the use of inductive reasoning, without the use of hedging, then the experts will immediately find weaknesses in your paper and be suspicious of any other claims you make.

Finally, it is not only important to have read into the different views on your subject; you must present any opposing claims to your own in order to remain objective. However, you must successfully refute these statements in order to ensure your own conclusions are successfully conveyed as the stronger claims.

3.2 – Critical thinking

Keywords

Assumption An idea that is believed or accepted as truth.

Biased In favour or against something, usually in a way that is considered unfair or based on personal opinion.

Evaluate Consider the advantages and disadvantages, review the strength of evidence on both sides. Use these details to reach an informed decision.

Fallacy An idea or conclusion based on false or misunderstood information.

Introduction

Trying to explain critical thinking in just a few pages is an almost impossible task. Therefore, this unit will only introduce what critical thinking is by putting it into contexts that should hopefully clear up the meaning behind this skill. Critical thinking plays an essential role in the evaluation of research, looking at others' arguments and coming to your own decisions about what ideas will form your essay.

Example of critical thinking

Every day you are surrounded by recommendations about what to buy, where to go, what to do, and how to do it. Advertisements are a classic example of persuasion. They are trying to get you to buy a particular product or to go to a certain place. This may be through humour, or by including your favourite celebrity, thereby using your emotions to 'trick' you into buying the items being advertised. However, do you ever stop and think why? Or, whether this product is the right product for you?

In some cases, especially if it is something expensive, you may stop and think about your options. You may go and read reviews, look at other products, and then make a decision based on all the information collected. In this example, you have used a form of critical thinking. You have explored all options and come to an informed decision before acting upon it.

How to think critically

You cannot just learn to think critically after reading a book or attending a series of lectures. Your brain is a muscle, and just like any other muscle in the body, you will need to train and practise to make it stronger. As everybody is different in the way he or she thinks, this unit can only offer suggestions on ways to approach critical thinking. One method, abbreviated to 'R.E.D', can be explained as follows.

Recognise assumptions

When you approach a new idea, a new topic or a new concept, you will need to read around the subject. Look and see what has already been written about this topic; look for the positive, the negative, and the neutral statements. The more you understand about the topic from every angle, the easier it will be to come to an informed decision.

Evaluate evidence

Look at all the evidence you have collected and see which sources are providing you with the most relevant information. But don't stop there; think about who wrote the text? Why did they write it? What evidence did they use? Does this evidence relate to the claim you are trying to make in your essay? Is it objective, or do you sense some **bias** in their ideas? Also, look out for **fallacies** in the information provided.

Draw a conclusion

This is the final step, and probably the one that will take the longest to master. It is important to remember that you should be avoiding any personal opinion. Make sure you are reaching a conclusion based on all the evidence you have evaluated. Even if you went into the research thinking the opposite, if you have genuinely evaluated the evidence and all sources point in a different direction, you need to present the logical conclusion.

Summary ✔

When presenting an argument in your essay, you should do this with integrity. This means you will make sure whatever you are suggesting or recommending to the reader is backed up with logical reasoning (through the use of supportive evidence). You should be objective and present everything you think the reader needs to know from all sides of the argument and provide enough detail so that they will hopefully arrive at the same position as you. The formation of your claims relies heavily on critical thinking, and therefore this skill is essential from the very start of the writing process.

Keywords

Clarity	The quality of being clear and easily understood.
Misinterpretations	Ideas that are incorrectly understood.
Presumption	An idea that is believed to be true but is not known for certain.
Presupposition	An idea that is created beforehand, with no intention to conduct research. Often influenced by a previous belief.
Relevance	The quality of an idea being related or appropriate.
Validity	The quality of being logical and reliable.

Introduction

Evaluating arguments in the research you read is a crucial part of critical thinking, and one particular factor you need to consider is whether a claim is formed around fallacies or not. Fallacies are lies or **misinterpretations** used to make an argument seem **valid**, and these fallacies can come in many different forms. This unit will provide you with some examples of common fallacies, along with brief explanations so you can begin to identify and avoid them during the collection of your research.

Types of fallacies

There is a very long list of fallacies you may encounter while conducting research. However, many of these can be separated into three categories: fallacies of irrelevance, presumption, and clarity. In all three categories, the final position has been reached through the use of poor reasoning, such as giving information that is off-topic or unrelated (*irrelevance*), relying on assumptions that are unnecessary and unsupported (*presumptions*), or through the use of language that confuses the reader (*clarity*).

Here are three basic questions to ask when evaluating arguments.

» **Relevance** – is the argument relevant to the topic?

» **Presumption** – is the argument assuming something that cannot be proven?

» **Clarity** – is the argument clear and easy to follow?

Fallacies of relevance

When an author wants to prove something, and they are struggling to find evidence that proves their idea to be truthful, it is easy to start giving ideas that are somewhat related, but not precisely on topic. There are many ways of doing this, but these kinds of fallacies can be grouped into the following three categories.

1. Arguments against the source

These kinds of fallacies are aimed at the author or the source of their evidence/ideas. The first example of this is to attack the person or organisation involved, resulting in the idea behind the claim not being addressed. This first example shows how an author will try to get the reader to side with their opinion by making the source look humiliated or evil:

> *The CEO released more lies into the newspapers today, saying that the company would not resort to layoffs in order to reduce financial losses for their investors. But this is a man who cannot be trusted and is heartless when it comes to the outcome of his employees.*

Additionally, an author may highlight the source's background, and use this to persuade the reader to think differently based their circumstances:

> *The president gave a statement today saying that he will raise more funds for the poor during his next term in office. He delivered this message while holidaying on his luxury yacht, which is probably funded by the country's taxes. How can a man who lives such a life of luxury be trusted with issues of providing benefits to the poor?*

Sometimes the author may avoid highlighting the issue at hand by using an example of someone or something else that is an even bigger issue. This use of comparison is a distraction technique, and is commonly used in advertisements:

> *Why buy an Apple MacBook computer? Well, Microsoft Windows has thousands of viruses out there targeted at collecting your personal data. In comparison to the alternatives, MacOS is far more secure, and your information will always remain safe.*

Finally, the author may choose to target where the information has come from, trying to pick a fault with the source, not with the actual idea itself. Again, this is a distraction used to present a negative representation of the information, without actually drawing a conclusion that is relevant:

> *Although there have been several reports showing the local mayor is corrupt, we cannot ignore that the media is biased and should not be trusted. The mayor has introduced so many positive improvements during his time in office, and the news outlets just want to provide an exciting story to increase their viewers.*

2. Appeals to emotions

These fallacies use emotions to persuade or change the reader's opinion. This fallacy is very broad and can be applied to almost any emotion. This first example given uses the emotion of fear to scare the reader into agreeing with the claim:

> *If the UK does not leave the European Union (EU), the population will have to pay even higher taxes and face many more immigrants coming into the country, some of which could be terrorists sneaking in to harm British citizens. Therefore, the population of the UK should vote to leave the EU.*

Another emotion that is often used to persuade readers is pity, presenting a situation where someone will be losing out, or be placed in a terrible position based on the issue being discussed:

> *Dr Adrian Smith should be awarded the Nobel Prize for Economic Sciences because he managed to come up with new theories in economics, even when he was going through though personal issues, such as the loss of his child and grandparents.*

Sometimes an idea will be forced onto the reader due to its popularity. This is a difficult one to spot as it is often accepted that if something is popular and believed by many, then it should just be accepted as truth:

> *The cars produced by Toyota receive some of the highest-rated reviews by critics and are currently the number one biggest selling brand. Therefore, Toyota produces the best cars for everyone.*

Similarly, an idea is present that is supported by an 'authoritative' figure. However, this person (or organisation) holds no authority on the issue and is being used as a sort of 'false idol' to support the argument. News outlets and magazines commonly use these fallacies, usually because the information has been researched by journalists, not specialists in the subject area:

> *During our visit, we interviewed the first customer James Lawson, who is head of the World Rollercoaster Fan Club, and he commented that 'Fantasy Land is by far the best value theme park in the country'.*

Finally, some sources will present information based on historic ideas and then compare these with current ones. This is a form of snobbery, looking down on what they believe to be a simple or underdeveloped idea:

> *New economic reforms that are similar to ones first introduced during the 1950s are to be reintroduced in the coming months. These reforms failed to make improvements the first time around, so what is the point of reapplying them to today's economically progressed society?*

3. Bending the truth

In these fallacies, the author's aim is to use false information, or to provide details that are exaggerated beyond the truth to add more persuasive power. To fully evaluate evidence like this, it is important to fact check. See if you can find the same or similar ideas presented in other sources:

> *Although they have yet to publish proof of their global tax payments, the fact that they are ranked as the world's most profitable company means that they cannot possibly have paid all of their taxes in full. There is no way this company has higher profits than other tech giants, such as Apple.*

There are times when a position is misrepresented, twisted or substituted to suit an argument that the author is trying to make. This is done by introducing a new 'pretend' argument. This technique also relies on the idea that the readers will not check the details further through additional research. In recent times, this has become synonymous with the term 'fake news':

> *The finance minister has decided to cut funding from the military to provide more financial support for healthcare systems. This is obviously a mistake; because of his decision, our country will become defenceless against any future attacks.*

Fallacies of presumption

These fallacies use a fact or idea that is assumed to be true, possibly a 'fallacy of popularity', and then use this point to try to prove something else to be true. These can be very complicated ideas that are stacked on top of each other, and even though the conclusion might make sense, it is all built on an idea that may not be true. These types of fallacies can be grouped into two categories.

1. Fallacies of presupposition

These fallacies occur when an argument is presented that has a conclusion built into it, without the use of any real logic or evidence for support.

The famous question, *'Which came first, the chicken or the egg?'* can usually be met with two answers. This is because an assumption has been made, *'chicken eggs cannot exist without chickens to lay them'* or *'chickens are born from eggs, so the first chicken had to come from an egg'*. Answers are given without being based on any real scientific evidence. Here is another example where no scientific evidence has been provided:

> *When left alone in a dark and reportedly haunted house, Sarah saw a ghostly figure. Nobody else was inside the house, and the doors were locked. Therefore, she must have experienced paranormal activity.*

It is often presented that there are only a limited number of choices available and that all other options are unacceptable or hidden from the reader. The presumption has been made that there is only a 'this or that' answer:

> *Based on the financial data presented, the company will either need to beg their investors for more money or close down their operations.*

Sometimes a similar fallacy occurs when there are two options, and an assumption is made that the answer is somewhere in-between, that there is an easy way to compromise:

> *The company want to sell their assets for around $2bn (USD), but their first offer was only $1bn (USD). Therefore, if they want to sell, they need to drop their asking price to at least $1.5bn (USD).*

Some arguments will conclude that something needs to be the way it is because that is more natural; it is what will happen without any aid or interference:

> *If someone is on his or her deathbed, the correct thing to do is let nature run its course. It is not the patient, the doctor, or anybody else's right to end a life earlier than nature intends. Euthanasia is unacceptable in any case.*

Finally, there are two more fallacies in this category that are presuming similar conclusions. When a part of a group has an issue (eg a store), then the whole group shares the same issue (eg the company):

> *VW Motors, one of the largest car manufacturing companies in Germany, has been accused of providing false emissions data on all their new models since 2012. This is typical of all Germany car manufacturers and will naturally result in a nationwide investigation.*

Or, when a larger group has issues (eg a company), it is because of a smaller part (eg a product):

> *Over the past ten years, Microsoft has seen a decrease in their profits. Their Windows operating system has been losing customers to other platforms. Therefore, this reduction of users is the reason behind their financial loss.*

2. Fallacies of induction

These fallacies usually include a conclusion that is drawn based on a sample. A very basic form of this is to think of flipping a coin 1,000 times. Sometimes the coin will be heads, and sometimes it will be tails. If you take a sample of 100 flips, and during that time you get 50 heads and 50 tails, then it is easy to presume that after 1,000 flips you will get 500 heads and 500 tails. Here is another example of using a sample to reach a conclusion:

> *75% of customers who flew with British Airways gave a five-star review of their overall flight experience. Therefore, when booking your next flight, be sure to choose British Airways.*

Another example of this is when there is a rule or idea that is accepted by many, and therefore must be applied to all (similar to the 'appeal to popularity' fallacy). This one is commonly used in advice:

> *It is often stated that cold things are bad for your stomach. Therefore, the cold drinks at Starbucks should be avoided to stay healthy. Always go for the hot drinks instead.*

Sometimes another example, specifically an analogy, is used to support the argument that is being made. Often these analogies are exaggerated, and wildly different from the original idea:

> *The government increasing taxes and taking more out of our monthly salaries is like being held up at gunpoint and robbed of our money.*

There are often conclusions drawn based on one thing causing another thing to happen, usually because these two things are sometimes associated with each other:

> *The number of terrorist attacks has increased since the government has allowed a more substantial number of immigrants into the country. Therefore, they are the ones who are committing these terrible crimes.*

Finally, statistical data can sometimes be used to support an argument. However, at times this data is presented using numbers that are often far too precise to be true/proven. This can sometimes occur due to the language used when presenting data:

> *The planet Earth was formed 4.54 billion years ago.*

Fallacies of clarity

This category of fallacies is related to how clear an argument is presented. Arguments can be confusing or difficult for the reader to follow, commonly due to the use of vague or ambiguous language. This is often a technique used by writers who wish to hide the fact they cannot support their argument, by trying to hide their true meaning with unnecessary language.

One example of this is to use ambiguous words or phrases to support a point, often resulting in a misleading argument. Including words that have multiple meanings is the most common technique used:

> *Books written about this software are rare, and rare books are expensive. So, if you manage to find one, you are going to have to pay a lot of money.*

Then there is the misinterpretation of an argument because a statement can be understood in different ways depending on where the accent (or the stress) has been placed in a sentence. This is often a problem when writers are using spoken language in their texts:

> *Huawei announced today that they managed to meet their sales target this year. Based on this, we can assume that Huawei usually struggles to meet their targets.*

The conclusion above has been reached because the first sentence has been interpreted with stress placed on the time frame 'this year', implying that this has not happened many times before.

Sometimes due to poor grammar, an argument can be completely misinterpreted. This is usually due to errors like run-on sentences, poor sentence composition, misplaced modifiers, or poor pronoun reference:

> *The most commonly received feedback from our customers is that they were happy with our wide selection of wines on offer, especially if they are old.*

Using fallacies in your writing?

When looking for evidence to support your claims, you should avoid using any source that is based on fallacies. Do not stray away from the idea you are trying to prove, do not assume something without relevant evidence, and do not confuse your reader with vague language. You do not want your own claims to become fallacies.

However, if there is a well-documented claim that you find to be based on fallacies, and this idea opposes your claim, you can use this evidence as a counter-argument. Then, during the rebuttal stage of your writing, you can highlight these fallacies to discredit the idea.

Summary ✔

Understanding what fallacies are, and how to identify them, is an essential skill to master. It plays an important role in the critical thinking required when conducting research, and again during the writing of your arguments. The only time fallacies should make an appearance in your essays is when you are refuting a counter-argument that is invalid due to fallacies.

Further reading

For more details about academic arguments and identifying fallacies, check out the following resource:

Larson, A., Hodge, J. and Perrin, C. (2010) *The Art of Argument*. 8th edn. Camp Hill, PA: Classical Academic Press.

Unit 04
Structure: Introductions

4.1 – General statements

Keywords

Hook	Something that is designed to grab attention.
Literature review	A report or summary of the key ideas that have been published relating to the topic being explored.
Thesis statement	A sentence provided in the introduction paragraph. This will outline the main claim of the entire essay.

Introduction

In academic writing, the structure of an essay is very important. There is no set structure that we must all follow; each writer has their own style, and with time, you will learn to write papers in your own unique way. However, throughout the next few units, this book will provide you with some guidelines to help form a cohesive structure that can be used in most academic essays.

Starting with the introduction paragraph, this section provides the reader with general information about the topic, why this is being discussed, and specific details about what the reader can expect to appear throughout the rest of the main body.

Opening sentences (hook)

The first few sentences of your introduction should grab your readers' attention; this is sometimes referred to as 'the hook'. This should be an interesting statement that makes the reader feel curious and willing to read the rest of your paper.

There are a few different options for what kind of hook can be used, and it depends on the type of paper you are writing. Below are a few choices to pick from.

» *Quotation* – this should be a line that has been spoken/written by a respected and well-known person connected to the topic. Be careful not to use proverbs, as these are often vague and unrelated to any specific topic.

» *Set a scene* – this is often more useful in reflective papers. Essentially, it involves writing a short description of a situation which the essay will be centred around.

» **Present facts or definitions** – provide the reader with some information they may not be familiar with or may hold misconceptions about.

Remember, this is still part of your general statements, and should not provide too many specifics about the main body of the essay. This information is reserved for later on in the introduction paragraph (known as the **thesis statement**).

 NOTE: A very common opening sentence used by EAP students is the phrase *'With the development of...'*, which is overused and disliked by many readers, making them feel bored before they have even started reading the paper. Therefore, you should not use this phrase at the start of your essay.

Background information

Following on from the opening sentence, you should continue to provide the reader with more general information about the broader topic. This should be background information that the reader may be unfamiliar with or information to help prepare the reader for the claim that will follow.

As an example, if you are writing a paper that will discuss the development of a company, do not waste words on giving a detailed history of the company. It would be far more useful to introduce the business environment the company is currently in or the most recent situation that has led to their current position (eg being the most successful in their industry).

The critical thing to remember is to start with statements that could be considered broad or general, with each following sentence becoming more specific than the last, narrowing down to your claim in the thesis statement (which is very focused and specific).

Introduce the wider topic

In much longer papers, you will usually be required to include something called a **literature review**. This is used to present what has currently been written about your topic. However, for shorter papers, introducing one or two key pieces of research relating to the topic should be sufficient enough. In your introduction, keep the use of research to a minimum, as you will go into more specific details in your main body paragraphs.

Explaining keywords and abbreviations

Something else that can be done in the general statements is to explain, define or clarify the meaning of specific keywords and abbreviations that will be used throughout the paper. Here are some examples of how this can be achieved:

> » *While many definitions of the term 'X' have been suggested, this paper will use the definition given by **AUTHOR (YEAR)** who saw it as…*
>
> » *Throughout this paper, the term 'X' will be used to refer to…*
>
> » *An issue faced by **English for Academic Purpose (EAP)** students is…*

Here are a few examples of general statements. These all include an opening sentence (hook), followed by background information that gradually becomes more specific. **NOTE**: There is no thesis statement provided in these examples, and therefore these are not complete introduction paragraphs.

Example 1

In September 2008, the world's financial sector was filled with horror as they watched the market collapse in front of their eyes. The banking system had been playing a dangerous game with people's money, and their luck had finally run out. The effect of this led to an economic crisis that was considered by many to be the worst since the 1930s, when the Great Depression hit hard.

Example 2

Brookfield (1996) once stated that 'Sometimes the last thing learners need is for their preferred learning style to be affirmed', adding that 'agreeing to let people learn only in a way that feels comfortable and familiar can restrict seriously their chance for development'. With Stephen Brookfield being considered a key figure in the area of teaching theory, this idea has been extensively written about from both sides of the argument. The dilemma is, should the aim be to present information to students and allow them to digest it in a way that is best for them, or is the real goal to push the students to develop themselves further.

Summary ✓

The introduction is essential for two reasons: grabbing the readers' attention, and easing them into the topic. You need to ensure that the first few sentences are interesting, but not too detailed. You do not want to scare the reader away with overly descriptive information, and you also do not want them to feel lost before they have even made it past the first paragraph. Providing a sample of background information, and an introduction to any key terminology will put their minds at ease and allow you to dive straight into your argument in the following main body paragraph.

References

Brookfield, S. (1996) 'Through the Lens of Learning: How Experiencing Difficult Learning Challenges and Changes Assumptions about Teaching', *To Improve the Academy*, 15, pp. 3–15.

4.2 – Thesis statements and essay maps

Keywords

Assertion	A confident statement in support of an idea.
Assignment brief	A document outlining details such as: the assessment task, deadlines, and how the work will be graded.
Cohesion	The flow of ideas connecting or uniting as a whole. Achieved through the use of keywords, linking phrases or grammar.
Cohesive device	Used in essays to link paragraphs (or sentences) together.
Controlling idea	The main idea that is covered in detail within a single main body paragraph.
Purpose statement	A sentence used to announce what is going to happen next. A way to informally tell the reader what to expect.
Skim read	A method of reading used to gather information quickly. This relies on cohesive devices to highlight what each area of an article focuses on.

Introduction

At the end of your introduction paragraph, you will need to provide a thesis statement. This is an essential part of academic papers. Without a clear thesis statement, it is impossible to present a cohesive piece of academic writing. The thesis statement is essentially the aim of your entire paper: what you want to achieve or what you want the readers to learn by the end.

Making your claim

The thesis statement is the part of the essay where your claim is first introduced to the reader. The way you present your claim can vary depending on the actual topic you are exploring, but in a basic form, you can think of it as stating that you are 'in favour' or 'against' a particular idea.

You cannot write an argumentative paper about being in support of both sides. Because of this, you need to make it very clear here in the thesis statement which side you support. Therefore, when writing your thesis, you can ask yourself: *What am I trying to prove by the end of this paper?*

Essay map

An essay map is a **cohesive device** that should be provided alongside the thesis statement. In the essay map, you should inform readers of your main body's **controlling ideas** (in the same order as the main body paragraphs). This is why it is called a 'map', because it provides directions, informing the reader of the route they will follow across your essay.

In some shorter essays, you may also be able to provide your essay map as part of your thesis statement. However, do avoid this if it will result in you creating a run-on sentence.

 NOTE: If you change the structure of your main body paragraphs, remember to rewrite your essay map to reflect these changes. It is essential for the **cohesion** of the paper. To avoid this, you could write the essay map after the entire paper has been written.

Writing a thesis statement

The way you form your thesis statement depends on how you received your topic in the **assignment brief**. If you are provided with a question that your tutor wishes you to answer, then it may just be a simple case of rephrasing your answer into a statement. However, if you are not given a specific question to answer, you will need to create the thesis statement based on your initial brainstorming session.

Thesis statement: From a question

If you are asked to answer a question such as '*What are the consequences of advertising through social media platforms?*', the thesis statement could be formed as follows.

The consequences of advertising on social media platforms are...

Advertising on social media platforms results in the following consequences...

Thesis statement: Without a question

If you are only provided with a general topic in the assignment brief, you will need to form your own 'question' to explore. This process can be done by following these steps.

» *Brainstorm your topic* – you may be asked to write about the topic of technology. You decide to focus on smartphones.

The use of smartphones.

» *Narrow the topic* – once research begins, you gather articles related to an increased use of smartphones among teenagers. This introduces an idea that could be argued.

> *Restricting teenagers' smartphone usage.*

» **Choose a position** – at this stage, you will need to begin forming a claim for your thesis statement. You could state that restricting teenagers' use of smartphones is necessary or unnecessary.

> *Teenagers should have restricted access to their smartphones.*

» **Make an assertion (based on your research)** – finally, revise your thesis into an assertive statement that clarifies your claim, and provides a little more detail about what aspect you will focus on (based on your initial research).

> *To protect the health and safety of teenagers, restrictions should be placed on their use of smartphones.*

Cohesion

Both the thesis statement and essay map play an essential role in the cohesion of your entire paper. These cohesive devices are there to tie your paper together; below is a diagram highlighting an essay's cohesive devices and how they are all connected.

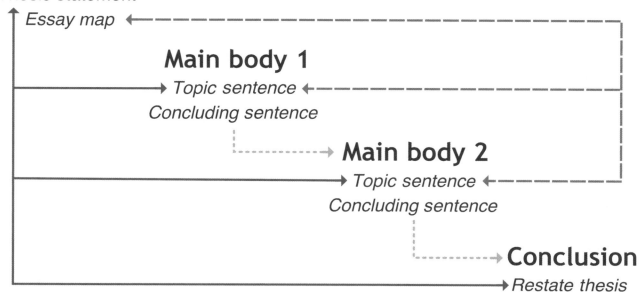

Thesis statement versus purpose statements

Although thesis and purpose statements are somewhat similar, the big difference is that purpose statements are slightly less formal. Their format reads more like an announcement, rather than a statement. Purpose statements tend to be seen as too direct and should be avoided in your writing. Here are some examples of how purpose statements usually start.

> *This paper will focus on/examine/give an account of...*
> *This essay critically examines/discusses/traces...*
> *This paper will review the research conducted on...*
> *This paper reviews the usefulness of...*
> *The aim of this paper is to determine/examine...*

Examples

In the following are some examples of thesis statements and essay maps. Following each example, you will find a few details about each of these cohesive devices and their purpose.

Example 1

To protect the health and safety of teenagers, restrictions should be placed on their use of smartphones. Limiting the amount of time spent using their smartphones will reduce the risk of both mental and physical symptoms, and further issues surrounding abuse or grooming can also be avoided by restricting access to specific applications.

The first sentence is the thesis statement (that was formed earlier in this unit). It provides a clear claim that surrounds the restriction of smartphone use among teenagers.

The sentence that follows is the essay map, outlining two main forms of restriction: limiting time and access to applications. For each of these restrictions, two ideas are given that highlight issues caused by unrestricted access to smartphones.

Depending on the word limit of the essay, you could write two main body paragraphs, with one focusing on why their time should be limited for health reasons, and one about restricting access to specific apps for safety purposes. Alternatively, you could write an essay with four main body paragraphs, one for each of the issues highlighted (the two relating to health and the two relating to safety).

Example 2

Because of the ever-growing child obesity problem in America, schools should be responsible for providing healthy alternatives to the current diets. This can be achieved through education on dietary requirements, adjusted cafeteria menus and changes in the options available through their vending machines.

Again, the first sentence is the thesis statement, which claims that schools should be held responsible for addressing the child obesity problem in the United States.

The following sentence is the essay map, which presents three controlling ideas: education on diet, adjustments to meals available in their cafeteria, and changing the items available in any on-campus vending machines. Each of these controlling ideas would be covered in their own main body paragraph.

Summary ✔

The introduction paragraph is an essential part of an essay's cohesion. The general statements guide the reader gently into the topic, while the thesis statement and essay map set up the structure which the entire essay is built upon. Without a clear claim being presented at the beginning, the reader will feel lost, and may even give up reading the essay due to confusion or lack of interest. The essay map serves as a guide for those who plan to read the essay in detail, but also serves as a useful for tool for those who which to **skim read** your article (a skill covered in elsewhere in this book).

Unit 05
Structure: main body paragraphs

5.1 – Topic sentences

Keywords

Cohesive device	Used in essays to link paragraphs (or sentences) together.
Purpose statement	A sentence used to announce what is going to happen next. A way to informally tell the reader what to expect.
Skim read	A method of reading used to gather information quickly. This relies on cohesive devices to highlight what each area of an article focuses on.
Supporting point	A statement that is provided in your main body paragraphs. This supports the claim and controlling idea provided in the topic sentence.
Thesis statement	A sentence provided in the introduction paragraph. This will outline the main claim of the entire essay.

Introduction

The largest section of your paper is made up of main body paragraphs. This is where all the ideas and information that support the thesis statement will be presented to the reader. In each main body paragraph, several elements need to be included to cover every idea in enough detail for the reader to fully understand.

Topic sentences are a form of **cohesive device** used to tie everything together, and maintain a continuous theme running throughout your paper. They are closely linked to the **thesis statement**, which is provided in the introduction paragraph, and informs the reader what to expect within each body paragraph.

Elements of a topic sentence

A topic sentence has two essential elements. The topic sentence needs to make a connection to the topic mentioned in the essay's claim (found in the *thesis statement*) and present a controlling idea for the body paragraph to focus on. It is also worth noting that these two elements can be given in any order.

English for Academic Purposes: A Handbook for Students

Controlling idea

The topic sentence is given at the start of a main body paragraph, and it must clearly state what the focus of that particular paragraph will be. This is done to guide the reader and inform them of what to expect in the following sentences.

Furthermore, for a reader who wishes to **skim read** your essay first (or quickly review it upon completion), topic sentences allow them to decide which paragraphs may offer them the most relevant information. This allows them to focus their attention on the areas of your essay they feel are the most important.

Topic

In order to improve cohesion, there is a need for some repetition throughout an essay (although this should be limited). In a topic sentence, keywords relating to the essay's claim should be provided. For example, if the essay makes a claim about the environment, then you would need to mention keywords relating to this subject in every topic sentence.

Writing a topic sentence

When writing a topic sentence, there are a few things to remember.

» **Make it interesting** – your topic sentence should grab the reader's attention and provide some new information that may raise questions in their mind.

» **Avoid general statements** – do not provide the reader with controlling ideas that are general or commonly known. For example, the information in this topic sentence is widely known: *'A dictionary contains the definitions of many words.'*

» **Be specific... but not too specific!** – you do need to provide enough detail for the reader to understand what the paragraph will focus on. However, do not give a topic sentence that is too specific, or you will not be able to explore the idea sufficiently.

» **Avoid announcements** – just like the thesis statement, avoid providing the reader with a **purpose statement**. Do not simply state: *'This paragraph will...'*

» **Make each one unique** – a common approach is to write each topic sentence with the same structure, starting each one with the same few opening words. This is repetitive and quite boring from a reader's perspective. Try to make each one different from the one used previously.

 NOTE: A topic sentence should only be one sentence in length. Splitting the topic sentence over two sentences will confuse the reader, and they may think the second sentence is actually a supporting point.

Examples

Here is an example of a thesis statement and essay map taken from an introduction paragraph.

* Example 1

Children's social interactions have been negatively affected by the increased use of technologies such as smartphones and tablets. Their attitude towards family members, their peers, and even strangers, has become increasingly disrespectful or even violent.

From this thesis statement, the essay's claim and controlling ideas can be identified.

» **Claim** – children's social interactions have been negatively affected... by technology.

» **Controlling ideas** – attitudes towards: 1) family members, 2) their peers, and 3) strangers.

These details can then be used to form the following topic sentence for main body paragraph 1.

Many family relationships have suffered a breakdown due to their children's increased access to technology.

The first controlling idea listed in the essay map is *'family members'*, and this has been addressed in the topic sentence through the term *'family relationships'*. The claim has also been mentioned by the terms *'suffered a breakdown'* (a negative effect) and *'children's increased access to technology'* (the topic of focus in this essay).

Again, here is an example of a thesis statement and essay map taken from an introduction.

* Example 2

The United Kingdom's decision to leave the European Union will result in several negative consequences for businesses. The biggest three issues surround the changes to trade regulations, restrictions on hiring foreign talent, and the devaluation of the pound.

From this thesis statement, the essay's claim and controlling ideas can be identified as follows.

» **Claim** – UK's decision to leave the EU... negative consequences for businesses.

» **Controlling ideas** – 1) changes to trade regulations, 2) hiring foreign talent, and 3) devaluation of the pound.

The following topic sentences can then be formed for the first main body paragraph.

The decision to leave the EU will result in new regulations that restrict foreign trade for businesses in the UK.

'Decision to leave the EU', *'restrict'*, and *'businesses in the UK'* are all phrases that refer back to the claim made during the thesis statement. *'New regulations'* is a term used to address the first controlling idea in the essay map: *'changes to trade regulations'*.

English for Academic Purposes: A Handbook for Students

Summary ✓

When working from a thesis statement and essay map, the topic sentences are quite easy to form. The main details are already there, they simply need to be rephrased into a sentence that informs the reader of the focus of each main body paragraph. Topic sentences not only guide the reader while they work their way through your essay, but also play an essential role for those who wish to skim through your paper. Although this cohesive device seems quite simple, it is actually one of the most essential components of an academic paper.

Keywords

Citation	Provided whenever evidence has been used in an essay. Part of the referencing process.
Conclusion	In forming an academic argument, this is the idea (or claim) that has been reached based on the evaluation of evidence.
Controlling idea	The main idea that is covered in detail within a single main body paragraph.
Essay map	A cohesive device that presents a summary of the main body's controlling ideas.
Evaluate	Consider the advantages and disadvantages, review the strength of evidence on both sides. Use these details to reach an informed decision.
Paraphrase	The presentation of others' ideas in your own words.
Premise(s)	In forming an academic argument, a premise(s) is a claim made by others (relating to the topic).
Quotation	Reported speech. A copy of somebody else's words (written or spoken), provided in 'quotation marks'.
Reasoning	In forming an academic argument, reasoning is used to explain or provide an explanation for how your conclusion was reached.
Redundancies	Words or phrases that do not add to or offer additional and useful information.
Referencing	The act of providing details that inform the reader where your evidence has been used and where the original text can be found.
Relevance	The quality of an idea being related or appropriate.
Reliable	Something that is considered to be high quality and trustworthy.
SED	Stands for supporting point, evidence and discussion. A structure used to present ideas in the main body paragraphs.
Summarising	The act of writing a brief description of a text's most important ideas (either evidence or sections of your own essay).
Topic sentence	A sentence given at the start of each main body paragraph to express the main idea that will be explored within it.

Introduction

The main body paragraphs are where the majority of your information will be presented to the reader. This is where ideas that support your thesis statement will be provided, followed by evidence to support these ideas, and a discussion of how this evidence is related to the claim you are making.

Supporting point, evidence and discussion (SED) structure

There are a few different approaches to how ideas are presented in an essay's main body paragraph, but one of the more commonly used structures is referred to as SED.

Supporting point

This is an idea, or more precisely, a **conclusion** that you have reached. This should be related to the **topic sentence** given at the beginning of the paragraph (both the essay's overall claim and the paragraph's **controlling idea**).

Supporting point
(Your idea / conclusion)

Evidence / example
(Others' ideas / premise)

Discussion
(Relevance / reasoning)

Returning to academic arguments (covered in Unit 3.1), the supporting point acts in the same way as the conclusion. This is an idea you have formed based on the evidence you have **evaluated** and decided to be both **relevant** and **reliable**.

Evidence/example

Sometimes referred to as either evidence or example. This should be information that has been collected during your research. You can present evidence as a **paraphrase**, **summary** or **quotation**. Again, in terms of academic arguments, the evidence serves the same purpose as the **premise(s)**.

Discussion

Once evidence has been provided, you may need to clarify its meaning, and more importantly, what is the relationship between the supporting point and the evidence? Moreover, how does this help prove your essay's thesis statement? Essentially, this is providing the reader with your **reasoning** (when forming academic arguments).

Repeat

In a well-supported academic paper, you will need to provide multiple supporting points, examples of evidence and discussions within each main body paragraph. This means once you have provided one *Supporting Point > Evidence > Discussion*, you will need to start all over again following the same pattern. This process is repeated as many times as you feel necessary until the controlling idea of the paragraph has been sufficiently supported.

SED then evidence and discussion (SEDED)

In some cases, you may not need to provide a second (or possibly third) supporting point. Here are two examples of when you can omit a supporting point.

» **More evidence is needed** – if you feel that a supporting point cannot be sufficiently supported by only one piece of evidence, then you may go straight into another piece of evidence after you have finished discussing the previous example.

» **Supporting points are similar or related** – if the next supporting point is similar or very closely related to the previous one, then you can include this point as part of the previous discussion. Thereby, this involves skipping straight into the relevant evidence without the need for a separate statement highlighting your supporting point.

 NOTE: Deliberately not providing a secondary supporting point is often done to avoid repetition or **redundancies**. However, as a beginner, this may be difficult to judge. Be sure to have your essay draft checked by a tutor if you are unsure.

Examples

Supporting point

The example of a thesis statement, essay map and topic sentence presented in the previous unit will be used as the starting point for this example of SED.

Thesis statement and essay map – children's social interactions have been negatively affected by the increased use of technologies such as smartphones and tablets. Their attitude towards family members, their peers, and even strangers, has become increasingly disrespectful or even violent.

Topic sentence – many family relationships have suffered a breakdown due to their children's increased access to technology.

Following on from this topic sentence, it is now time to present an idea that supports this controlling idea. In the following is a supporting point that claims that if children have a deeper understanding of technology, then it will negatively affect the relationship with their parents.

Because children have grown up with access to technology from an early age, they often know more about these devices than their parents do.

Evidence/example

Once the supporting point has been provided, the next step is to present some evidence. This should be provided from trusted and reliable sources, and also written carefully into your paragraph using the correct method of paraphrasing, summarising or quotation. This example is continued in the following.

Many family relationships have suffered a breakdown due to their children's increased access to technology. Because children have grown up with access to technology from an early age, they often know more about these devices than their parents do. Subrahmanyam et al. (2001) suggest that this developed understanding of technology results in the child becoming a teacher to their parents.

Following on from the supporting point, a piece of evidence has been paraphrased into the paragraph. Alongside this evidence is information telling you that this was taken from research conducted by Subrahmanyam and his colleagues, which was published in an article back in 2001. This information is called a **citation**, which is a part of **referencing**.

Discussion

At this point, if the paragraph moved on to a new supporting point, the reader would be left confused. If the child teaches their parents how to use these devices, what effect will that have on their relationship? Why is this a negative thing? The example is continued in the following.

> *Many family relationships have suffered a breakdown due to their children's increased access to technology. Because children have grown up with access to technology from an early age, they often know more about these devices than their parents do. Subrahmanyam et al. (2001) suggest that this developed understanding of technology results in the child becoming a teacher to their parents. This role reversal, where the child becomes a more authoritative figure, can lead to a loss of respect for their parents.*

Now that the evidence has been explained by the author, you can clearly see that the reason for this idea and this piece of evidence is to show: 'child = teacher, parent = student'. This can then lead to the parents no longer being respected by their children. Therefore, the child thinks they know more than their parents and could result in the child thinking they can make better decisions or choices in their own lives.

A sentence for each section? Not necessarily!

Each part of SED does not have to be a single sentence. For some parts, such as the discussion, you may need to provide several sentences to successfully convey the relevance and reasoning. Similarly, two parts can actually overlap into a single sentence, which often happens when a supporting point leads straight into a piece of evidence. Look at the example which is continued in the following.

> *Many family relationships have suffered a breakdown due to their children's increased access to technology. Because children have grown up with access to technology from an early age, they often know more about these devices than their parents do. Subrahmanyam et al. (2001) suggest that this developed understanding of technology results in the child becoming a teacher to their parents. This role reversal, where the child becomes a more authoritative figure, can lead to a loss of respect for their parents. Moreover, users on many applications use anonymous screennames, meaning a child will communicate with both children and adults in an equal manner (Subrahmanyam et al., 2001). Consequently, children will expect the same treatment in real life. This means they will address their parents in a more casual manner, and if they disagree with a parent's comment, the child may merely 'block' their parent's instructions.*

In this example, you can see that the first of these newly added sentences is acting as both the supporting point and a piece of evidence. Then, the next two sentences are providing a discussion to establish both the relevance and reasoning behind the previous supporting point and evidence.

Summary ✔

The SED structure is a great starting point for introducing ideas in an academic paper. There are several alternatives, and even SED can be altered depending on the assessment task. However, for beginners, this method is useful for gaining confidence in your own writing. Once you have grasped the ability to express your ideas clearly using this method, you can then begin to experiment, and further develop your writing approach in the main body paragraphs.

References

Subrahmanyam, K. et al. (2001) 'The Impact of Computer Use on Children's and Adolescents' Development', *Applied Developmental Psychology*, 22, pp. 7–30.

5.3 – Concluding sentences

Keywords

Cohesive device	Used in essays to link paragraphs (or sentences) together.
Controlling idea	The main idea that is covered in detail within a single main body paragraph.
Essay map	A cohesive device that presents a summary of the main body's controlling ideas.
SED	Stands for supporting point, evidence and discussion. A structure used to present ideas in the main body paragraphs.
Skim read	A method of reading used to gather information quickly. This relies on cohesive devices to highlight what each area of an article focuses on.

Introduction

Once the supporting point, evidence and discussion (**SED**) structure has been followed, the concluding sentence is used to finish off a main body paragraph. This is another **cohesive device** used to help the reader follow the ideas presented in your essay. Furthermore, a concluding sentence is given to ensure that main body paragraphs do not finish on a discussion or a piece of evidence. Doing so will result in an abrupt ending to your paragraph that will leave your reader feeling unsatisfied.

Cohesion between paragraphs

The ultimate purpose of a concluding sentence is to let the reader know that the current main body paragraph is coming to an end, informing the reader that you have sufficiently supported the current **controlling idea**.

However, a secondary purpose of the concluding sentence is to provide a transition into the next main body paragraph. This is done by providing some keywords that relate to the controlling idea of the following paragraph, creating a small (*cohesive*) link to the next paragraph.

Remember to refer to the **essay map** mentioned in your introduction paragraph. Following on from the example main body paragraph presented in the previous unit, the following concluding sentence will provide a link to the next main body paragraph, which has the controlling idea of 'peer interactions'.

*...Meaning they will address their parents in a more casual manner, and if they disagree with a parent's comment, the child may merely 'block' their parent's instructions. **Overall, these situations reinforce a negative attitude that not only affects the relationships among family members, but also causes issues surrounding their interactions with classmates and friends.***

Final main body paragraph

When the final main body paragraph has been reached, there is no possible way to provide a transition as the next paragraph will be the conclusion. Therefore, you only need to provide a sentence that signals the end of the current main body paragraph. Following on from the previous example, the next example shows how a concluding sentence could be provided for the final main body paragraph based on the controlling idea 'attitudes towards strangers'.

> *...With all these points taken into consideration, it is evident that children who spend an extended amount of time using devices such as smartphones and tablets will indeed exhibit an increased tendency to lash out and potentially cause harm to those around them, including innocent bystanders.*

This example wraps up the paragraph and reaffirms what controlling idea was given at the beginning of the paragraph. There are no details indicating a paragraph will follow, as the sentence only relates to the idea of violent behaviour towards strangers.

Summary ✔

This part of a main body paragraph is often forgotten about but does actually play an important role in signalling when a controlling idea has been explored to its fullest. The slight hint at what the next paragraph will focus on is also useful for those who are reading through your essay in detail, as well as those who wish to **skim read** for areas of the essay to focus on while previewing or reviewing.

5.4 – Cohesion

Keywords

Cohesive device	Used in essays to link paragraphs (or sentences) together.
Concluding sentence	Used to signal that the current idea has been explored in sufficient detail.
Discourse marker	Words or phrases used to connect different sentences or clauses.
Thesis statement	A sentence provided in the introduction paragraph. This will outline the main claim of the entire essay.
Topic sentence	A sentence given at the start of each main body paragraph to express the main idea that will be explored within it.

Introduction

Throughout the book so far, especially within this set of units, the word 'cohesion' has been mentioned on several occasions. Academic papers contain elements of cohesion running throughout, and as the main body paragraphs are the largest section, it is important to use as many elements of cohesion as possible to help your readers stay focused.

Cohesive devices

Thesis statements, **topic sentences**, and **concluding sentences** are just some of the cohesive devices mentioned throughout this book. These are used to connect every paragraph, making sure the paper stays on topic, and the reader is following along with ease.

However, cohesion is not only about connecting paragraphs; it is also important to think about how information is connected within each paragraph. There are many different grammatical rules that can be used to make connections, but there are a few specific elements that can be used to increase cohesion effectively.

Discourse markers

Discourse markers are useful for connecting individual sentences. They signal what details are about to follow on from the previous sentence – whether it be adding further information, presenting a contrasting or opposing idea, or introducing an entirely new idea that moves on from the previous one. However, discourse markers are not only limited to connecting separate sentences, as they can also be used within a sentence to connect two clauses.

Being explicit in your writing, which includes being cohesive, is one of the features of academic writing.

Table of discourse markers

Explicit use	Discourse marker	Explicit use	Discourse marker
Giving more information	*In addition...* *Additionally...* *Moreover...* *Furthermore...*	**Comparing ideas**	*Likewise...* *Similarly...* *Equally...* *In the same way...*
Giving examples	*For example...* *For instance...* *Namely...* *Such as...*	**Concession**	*Of course...* *Admittedly...* *Obviously...*
Summarising	*In summary...* *In conclusion...* *In short...* *In brief...*	**Emphasising**	*In particular...* *Especially...* *Above all...* *Significantly...*
Sequencing ideas	*First...* *Second...* *Finally...* *The former...* *The latter...* *Meanwhile...* *Subsequently...*	**Clarifying**	*To put it another way...* *In other words...* *That is to say...*
Giving a reason	*Due to the fact that...* *Owing to the fact that...* *Because of...* *Since...*	**Speaking generally**	*Generally...* *In general...* *Typically...*
Cause and effect	*Therefore...* *Consequently...* *Thus...* *Hence...*	**Parallel time**	*At the same time...* *Simultaneously...* *Meanwhile...* *In the meantime...*
Contrasting ideas (balanced, with no emphasis)	*Alternatively...* *Then again...*	**Changing the subject**	*Incidentally...*
Contrasting ideas (emphasising difference)	*However...* *Whereas...* *Conversely...* *In theory...* *In practice...*	**Returning to the previous subject**	*As mentioned earlier...* *As mentioned previously...*

NOTE: Looking at examples or finding a list of discourse markers is not going to help you improve your writing, as they work differently depending on the context. Therefore, the only way to improve your use of discourse markers is to read more and pay attention to their use in others' work.

Giving more information

There are several discourse markers used when providing further information, thus expressing that the current idea is still being explored.

> *To gain more customers, they need to provide a broader range of options. **Moreover**, their prices will need to be adjusted to effectively compete in the current market.*

Giving examples

Sometimes an idea has been presented, but an example is needed to add clarity. This type of discourse marker is used to highlight that an example is being presented relating to the current idea.

> *The number of tourists visiting Asian countries has massively increased over the past ten years. **For instance**, China has seen its inbound tourism figures multiply by a factor of ten since 2006.*

Summarising

This type of discourse marker is useful for providing discussion or clarification. Furthermore, they can also be useful indicators that a concluding sentence (or even a concluding paragraph) is about to be given.

> *...team-building and creative thinking. **In summary**, the key to becoming a successful leader is through the development of critical skills.*

Sequencing ideas

Providing a bullet list of items or ideas in academic essays is often seen as poor practice. Therefore, when a list of ideas needs to be presented, this should be done through detailed sentences that make efficient use of sequencing.

> ***First**, there needs to be an increased number of customers attending the events to provide enough income to cover the running costs. **Second**, with an increase in customers comes a demand for higher staff numbers, which in turn increases running costs. **Finally**, the venue itself will need to...*

Summary ✔

Cohesion is vital for constructing an essay that is logical and easy for the readers to follow. It is for this same reason that cohesion often accounts for a significant part of your grade, as your tutors will not only be checking to see that you can provide ideas in a sensible order, but that you can also provide links between and within paragraphs. Be sure to use the cohesive devices mentioned throughout these units on structure, but do not forget to use the other elements of cohesion such as discourse makers to enhance the links between the different ideas and statements made in your papers.

Unit 06
Structure: Conclusions

6.1 – Elements of a conclusion

Keywords

Discourse marker	Words or phrases used to connect different sentences or clauses.
Essay map	A cohesive device that presents a summary of the main body's controlling ideas.
Hedging	Cautious language that is used when presenting ideas that have some level of doubt regarding the validity or certainty.
Paraphrase	The presentation of others' ideas in your own words. Or, in the case of conclusions, taking your ideas and rephrasing them to avoid repetition.
Thesis statement	A sentence provided in the introduction paragraph. This will outline the main claim of the entire essay.

Introduction

The conclusion is the final paragraph of an essay; it is your last chance to make an impression on the reader. It is also your final opportunity to make sure the reader has fully understood your argument and that your claim has been successfully explored. Just as the introduction is important for giving the reader a good first impression, the conclusion is essential for leaving the reader with a lasting impression. If your paper successfully informs and educates your readers, they will be more likely to read your articles in the future.

Structuring a conclusion

A conclusion can be broken down into four elements. Below is a brief introduction to the order in which these are usually presented.

» **Summarising discourse marker** – the opening of your conclusion should signal that your essay is coming to an end. This can be done by starting the conclusion with a summarising discourse marker.

» **Restate claim** – you will need to remind the reader of the original claim made in your **thesis statement**. This should not be repeated word for word, but instead restated.

» **Summary** – following this, you will need to provide a summary of the main ideas and arguments raised throughout the main body paragraphs.

» **Final idea** – at the very end of your conclusion, you should provide a statement that will leave your reader satisfied and eager to learn more about the topic. This can be provided as a suggestion on ways to improve a particular situation or a prediction of what may happen in the not-too-distant future.

 NOTE: Avoid using the discourse marker 'In a word...' This is often seen as inappropriate, as it is commonly used to summarise a situation down to a single word. Conclusions are not just one word, and by using this phrase, you may sometimes annoy your readers.

Summarising discourse marker

In Unit 5.4, you were provided with a table of discourse markers that can be used throughout your papers. However, a summarising discourse marker can be a useful opener to your concluding paragraph. By starting with one of the following, your reader will already expect this paragraph to contain your concluding statements.

In conclusion...	To conclude...	In summary...	To summarise...
To sum up...	In short...	All in all...	On the whole...

Restate claim

Before you summarise the key points of the essay, it is a good idea to restate the essay's overall claim that you presented in your thesis statement. However, do not simply copy and paste the thesis statement from the introduction. You should **paraphrase** these details to present your claim in a less repetitive manner.

Summary

The main body paragraphs should be full of interesting ideas, far too many for the reader to remember by the time they reach the end of the paper. Therefore, a reminder of the journey taken through the essay will need to be provided. This does not mean that everything needs to be reviewed, but at least one of the leading ideas raised in each main body paragraph would be worth summarising for the reader.

The method of summarising is covered in Unit 9.3, but it is worth noting that as a guide for conclusions, you should be providing roughly one to two sentences of summary per main body paragraph.

 NOTE: Another critical thing to remember is that there should be no new information provided in your summary. There is no need to give any new ideas or evidence as all of your main ideas should have been provided in your essay's main body paragraphs.

Final idea

The last few sentences of your paper are significant, as it is the final impression you will leave on your reader. The purpose of the final idea is to impress and present something for the reader to continue their interest in the topic after they have finished reading your paper. Ideally, it should leave them with a desire to explore further into the topic. Typically, the final idea can contain one of the following.

» **Suggestion** – the point of a suggestion is to give the reader of the paper something to think about regarding change. For example, if your paper is based on the structure and workings of a company, then the suggestion may propose a change in their management or advertising.

» **Prediction** – based on the points you have raised throughout your essay, give the reader an idea of what may happen in the future. This could be a prediction surrounding the idea that something will change, or what may happen if nothing changes. As this is about the future, be sure to use **hedging**, as this may not be certain to happen.

Conclusion example

Here is an example of a thesis statement, essay map and conclusion based on a topic exploring the difficulties students face when moving to university.

> ***Thesis statement and essay map** – Students are facing high levels of pressure when they move away from home to start university. They are ill-equipped with the necessary skills of living on a budget, managing their own time, and preparing a healthy and balanced diet.*

> ***Conclusion** – To summarise, as with anyone who moves on and leaves their comforts and security behind, it is understandable that students meet many difficulties when they leave home. As well as studying for their chosen degree, students have to learn many life lessons that they have relied on their parents to do for them in the past, such as managing time and money. Other life skills such as cooking and cleaning can vary depending on a child's upbringing, but there is still a growing concern that many students feel: doing it alone will lead to many mistakes. It is commonly known that these skills need to be learnt from trial and error. However, one suggestion is that more educational institutes should set up student support, which can help teach students some of these skills, possibly during their induction week, but should be available throughout their studies as these difficulties can arise at any time.*

Summary ✔

The essential information provided in a concluding paragraph is quite easy to form, as it is entirely based on the details in the main body of your essay. The challenging aspect is making sure you are not merely repeating the ideas word for word. Using a combination of summarising and paraphrasing your own words should be sufficient in achieving this, but do not forget to provide a final idea that will leave a lasting impression on the reader. This also can be quite challenging and should certainly be an area where you can ask others for feedback; see if others agree that your final idea is interesting or thought-provoking.

Keywords

Assignment brief	A document outlining details such as: the assessment task, deadlines, and how the work will be graded.
Discourse marker	Words or phrases used to connect different sentences or clauses.
Hedging	Cautious language that is used when presenting ideas that have some level of doubt regarding the validity or certainty.
Paraphrase	The presentation of others' ideas in your own words. Or, in the case of conclusions, taking your ideas and rephrasing them to avoid repetition.
Prediction	A statement that presents a situation that is likely to happen in the future based on the research you have conducted.
Suggestion	A statement that makes a recommendation for change based on the research you have conducted.
Summarising	The act of writing a brief description of a text's most important ideas (either evidence or sections of your own essay).

Introduction

Three of the elements included in the conclusion paragraph are explored to some degree across several units in this book; **discourse makers** are covered in Unit 5.4, restating your claim using **paraphrasing** can be located in Unit 9.2, and **summarising** can be found in Unit 9.3. However, details on what needs to be considered while writing the final idea require some further explanation.

Leave your reader wanting more

The difficulty here is finding the right balance between leaving your reader with a desire to learn more about the topic and presenting unanswered questions. Your main body paragraphs should have explored your claim and provided answers to any possible questions that may have been raised while providing evidence and discussions.

However, there may have been some ideas that were not fully explored for various reasons. For example, one of your ideas may have centred around a relatively recent concept, meaning there is very little evidence to support this point. Alternatively, the word limit provided in your **assignment brief** may also be restricting your ability to explore complex ideas in sufficient detail.

Therefore, your final idea can be used to provide a direction for your readers to explore after completing your essay, via further reading and areas for extended research.

Types of final ideas

The way you finish your paper can vary depending on the type of essay you are writing, or even the subject of focus. However, there are two commonly used final ideas in academic papers: suggestions or predictions.

Suggestions

Sometimes the topic you have written about will highlight areas where changes may be necessary for development. Therefore, a good way to finish the essay is by providing a recommendation, focusing on a specific idea that would help to improve a situation.

Alternatively, you may also want to suggest particular areas that need further investigation: either by yourself, someone else in the same field of study, or as further reading for anyone who may be interested after completing your essay.

NOTE: At this stage, it may feel like you are speaking directly to the reader but remember that you can never be sure who your audience is going to be. Therefore, you need to avoid the use of any second-person pronouns (eg you).

Prediction

Through researching your topic, you may have encountered several predictions. These ideas may point towards a positive or negative outcome that is due to happen in the coming years. You may have mentioned some of these points briefly within your main body, but in your final idea, you can present which outcome is more likely to happen. You could even predict in roughly how many years this may begin to take effect.

It is important to remember that when raising ideas about the future, there is always a level of uncertainty. Most of the time, predictions are based on patterns and comparisons to similar situations in the past. Therefore, if you decide to present a prediction as your final idea you must use **hedging** to emphasise that this idea is not guaranteed to happen.

NOTE: Predictions should provide some specific details regarding the outcome. Avoid writing vague statements that say, *'In the future, everything will be fine'* or *'If more attention is not paid to our children's behaviour, the next few years will be difficult'* – what exactly is meant by 'fine' or 'difficult'?

Summary ✔

The final idea is the last sentence of your essay, and this is your final chance to impress the reader. Remember to provide information that is relevant to the ideas explored in your main body paragraphs, and do not merely repeat something you have already stated earlier on in the essay. Get your readers interested in the subject and encourage them to read more or continue to follow the subject after they have finished your paper.

Unit 07
Finding evidence

7.1 – Types of sources

Keywords

e-Book	An electronic version of a book.
e-Journal	An electronic version of a journal.
Peer-reviewed	An article that has been read by experts (in the area/topic of discussion) and approved before being published.
Reliability	The quality of being trustworthy and accurate.
Validated	Checked and confirmed, or at least assumed by many, to be true facts.

Introduction

For many students, the internet is often seen as the only place to locate evidence, and although many other types of sources have found new homes in a digital form, there is still a range of other sources that should not be ignored. Each type of source has its advantages and disadvantages, and if you want to produce a well-supported and balanced paper, a variety of sources will need to be used as evidence throughout your essay.

Published material

It used to be that most published material came in the form of printed media, and this was usually an indicator of something being somewhat more reliable than the average digital source (which is usually just a website). However, nowadays you can often find a digital version of most printed sources. Here are some examples of sources that usually go through some form of physical publication.

Books

Previously, for a book to be published, the author's work had to be checked by several different specialists in the same field. This usually means that the author's opinions are **validated** or at least appreciated by their peers. Nowadays, there has been a rise in the number of self-published titles, so it is important to pay attention to the publishing company that prints the book. If a book is not distributed by a well-established publisher, the **reliability** of the book becomes questionable.

One advantage of books is they often clearly list who the author is, so it is easy for you to research into other works written by the same author. The two biggest disadvantages to books are that they can sometimes become outdated quickly and they may be expensive, especially if the book needs to be imported from overseas.

Newspapers

There are two key types of newspapers: broadsheets and tabloids. Broadsheet newspapers tend to have more formal language, focused social and business topics, and provide detailed accounts of their sources. Tabloids, on the other hand, tend to focus on entertainment, gossip and general news stories. Both types of newspapers are facing difficult times and are considered a dying media. Many have switched to online sources but can sometimes request a payment to read the entire article.

Magazines

These can be very similar to newspapers in many respects, but the one advantage magazines have is that their writers tend to be specialised in the topic of the magazine. Although some sections of a newspaper may have dedicated journalists, often some of the main news articles are written by people who have to research the topic as they write, meaning they can often make mistakes or misinterpret facts.

Magazines usually have a focused topic, which can also help with locating useful research for your paper. However, as with newspapers, this is considered a dying media, with many of the larger magazine companies switching their focus towards an online presence.

Journals

For many, journals are considered to be the most academic and reliable example of a published source. A journal is a collection of articles written by professionals, lecturers or high-levelled students in their respective fields. This means that the authors of journal articles have a deep understanding of the topic being discussed.

Furthermore, journals are often **peer-reviewed**, which means that nothing gets printed in a journal until members of their peers have read and agreed that the article is suitable to be shared with a wider audience. However, this does not guarantee that every detail included in an article is correct. You will still need to read around the subject and look for journals that present different perspectives on a particular topic.

Probably the two biggest disadvantages with journals are their cost and, for EAP students, the language used. Luckily, the high cost of journals is often covered by universities, as they will often provide printed copies in their libraries. Additionally, this is another media that has moved towards electronic formats, meaning they can also be located in your university's e-library. However, the language issue remains, as they are written in very formal and technical language that will require more care and attention by EAP students.

The internet

Unfortunately, as the internet is so expansive, it is a huge mess of news, encyclopaedia entries, blogs, social media posts, and numerous pages of useless information. It is critical to be selective in your choice of digital texts, with often the best options being digital versions of the printed media mentioned above (especially **e-books** and **e-journals**).

Summary ✓

It is easy to rely on the internet for your research, but do not limit yourself. Be sure to spend some time in your campus or local library, as there are still plenty of useful sources that are only available in printed form. Even if you do use the internet, be sure to look into electronic versions of printed material, such as e-books or e-journals. Do not be distracted by the availability of general websites, especially news articles published online. These may be easier to find and understand, but their reliability can be questionable.

Keywords

Biased	In favour or against something, usually in a way that is considered unfair or based on personal opinion.
Fallacy	An idea or conclusion based on false or misunderstood information.
Opinion	A point of view on a subject that is not generally based on research.
Primary source	Evidence that you have personally collected through questionnaires, real-world observations, or interviews.
Quotation	Reported speech. A copy of somebody else's words (written or spoken), provided in 'quotation marks'.
Reliability	The quality of being trustworthy and accurate.
Secondary source	Evidence that is presented by others.
Validity	The quality of being logical and reliable.

Introduction

Collecting information from a wide range of sources is an excellent way to start your research. However, once you have gathered this information, you will also need to identify the different types of evidence that are available. Each of these different types have their own strengths and weaknesses, and it is essential to understand these before deciding if and how you will present them.

Fact

If you can support your ideas with facts, then your arguments will be extremely convincing. These can come from the sources you read (**secondary sources**) or through observation (**primary source**). To be considered as a fact, the information cannot be disputed or shown to be based on **fallacies**.

* Example

Microsoft was founded on the 4th April 1975.
London is the capital of the United Kingdom.
Monday always comes before Tuesday.

Opinion

Facts are sometimes confused with 'common knowledge' or even '**opinions**'. These are ideas that are believed by many but are difficult to prove, usually due to a lack of support. Additionally, these are often ideas that are based on misinterpretations to reach a conclusion.

> ## * Example
>
> *Apple makes the best computers in the world.*
> *Alcohol is bad for society.*
> *Cats are the best pet for modern families.*

Statistics

Providing statistics and numerical data is a great way to support your arguments. This kind of information has been collected through surveys or observations. However, be sure to check the **reliability** of this data and pay attention to their sample size (ie how many people did they ask?).

> ## * Example
>
> *In 2016, over 65% of the UK's citizens were considered to be overweight.*
> *In the US, the number of unemployed increased by 19,000 to 6.65 million.*
> *Tesla is now producing an average of 2,000 cars per week.*

Quotation

The use of quotations should be kept to a minimum, but there are some instances where these can provide sufficient support. Try to look out for information that has been presented by experts or an authoritative figure, as their names alongside the quotation will add further **validity** to your argument. More details on the use of quotations can be found in Unit 9.5.

 NOTE: Be extremely careful who the authoritative figure is, and what point they are trying to make. For example, if you choose to use a CEO of a company, their information may be **biased**.

Use of examples

Sometimes you will need to provide an account of how something happened, or possibly a common occurrence. In reflective papers, this would usually come from personal experience. However, for an argumentative paper, you will need to look for an external source that details how something is done or has happened in the past.

Use of evidence

Evidence can be used at various points throughout your paper, and in each case, you will need to provide this information for different purposes. The following table includes the types of evidence listed in this unit and a suggestion on where you may be able to use them in your essay.

Purpose	Type of evidence
Background information	Facts Examples (What happened?)
Giving examples	Facts Statistics Examples
Supportive commentary	Quotations (Opinions, assumptions, and theories of experts or respectable figures)

More details regarding the use of evidence, and how to present this information within your essay, can be found in Unit 9.

Summary ✔

To effectively provide support for your arguments, you will need to understand the difference between sources and the types of evidence that can be found within them. Try to provide a variety of evidence types throughout your work and be sure to pay attention to when each type would be more effective. Especially monitor your use of quotations, as these should not be overused, and are more effective if they are provided alongside another type of evidence (such as facts, statistics or examples).

7.3 – Conducting research

Keywords

Brainstorm	The act of gathering and creating ideas.
Reference	A mention or link to something. For example, a reference number is used to identify an item, such as a book.
Search string	The words or phrases typed into a search bar.
Synonym	Words or phrases that have the same meaning.

Introduction

The approach to research is constantly developing, and it can vary depending on the subject you are studying. For most, the starting point will be the library, while others may need to go out and observe, or it may be a case of browsing the internet to find the right sources for the assessment task. Regardless of which route you take, make sure you plan and **brainstorm** ideas first, as this will narrow down your searches.

Reading lists

Many courses will provide you with a list of recommended reading material, which is usually located in the course or module handbook. This is a great place to start, as it will give you an idea of what texts have been considered by your tutors while writing assignments and class material. If you are struggling to find any of the items listed, try looking for other material by the same authors or with similar titles.

Using the library

As soon as you arrive, make use of the library catalogues, which nowadays are usually electronic. You can do this alone, or with the aid of one of the librarians. Many libraries also offer specialist collections for your subject, as well as indexes for national collections. Furthermore, many libraries provide a search function on their website, so you can even do a search from home before arriving.

The library is not only an excellent place to do research, but also one of the best places to get some work done. It is a quiet environment with very few distractions, and if you get stuck for ideas, you can take a walk around and find inspiration from other areas you may have never considered before.

There are some differences between libraries, however; you may want to pay attention to the following tips.

» Fiction is arranged in alphabetical order by the author's surname.

» Reference books are arranged by subject, with each subject being given a number that is provided on the spine of the book.

» You can find a book's **reference** number by looking it up in the library's catalogue.

» All the books on a given subject are grouped together on the shelves.

Journals usually contain the latest research for your subject, as well as literature reviews. Most journal articles have a short abstract at the beginning that tells you what the articles are about. Browsing through the abstracts and reviews helps to keep you up to date on the subject.

In the majority of university courses, you will be expected to refer to journal articles in most assignments. Journals are published at regular intervals during the year, just like magazines. They are collected into numbered volumes, usually one for each year.

Using search engines

When using a search engine, you may find that you receive millions of pages relating to your topic, and therefore you may waste time reading through many irrelevant pages.

A common mistake is to ask a search engine the answer to a question. As it is essentially a machine, it does not read every word you type; it simply tries to locate the keywords in your **search string**. Most of the time it does a great job of ignoring the extra words you have typed in, but sometimes those extra words can cause the search engine to return additional sources that may distract you from your search aim.

Ideally, when using a search engine, you should only provide keywords. If you use more specific keywords, the search engine will return fewer results, thereby reducing the amount of time wasted on clicking through hundreds of websites. For example, here is a list of searches conducted on the word 'referencing'.

Search string	Referencing	Harvard referencing	Harvard referencing system
Number of results	12,300,000	689,000	328,000

To save yourself some time and effort, choose your search string carefully.

» Remove any unnecessary words (eg *the*, *of*, and *it*).

» Focus on the keywords relating to your subject. If another subject shares a keyword with yours, try to add another word that narrows down the results.

» Try to find **synonyms** for some of your keywords (eg *apartment* and *flat*).

Advanced search and search operators

Many search engines have an advanced search function, which is often located on their homepage. However, if you cannot immediately find this, type 'Advance Search' into the search engine, and the top result should be a link to the relevant page.

Advance searches are useful for the following.

» Focusing on, or ignoring, specific keywords located on web pages.

» Searching for data or numbers between a specific range (eg *between $300 and $600*).

» Returning results in a specific language.

» Returning results from specific domains (eg *.co.uk, .cn, .edu, .ac.uk*).

» Returning websites that host specific file types (eg *PDF, .docx, .ppt*).

» Searching for results published after a certain date to access the most recent research.

For search engines that do not provide an advanced search function, you can make use of some of the following operators to help narrow down your search string through the usual search bar.

Search operator	How to use it?
– **(Dash symbol)**	Use the dash symbol before a word or site to exclude it from the results: eg *Panda –Sichuan*
" " **(Quotation marks)**	Quotation marks around phrases return pages with words appearing in that order (next to each other on the page): eg *"plagiarism in university"*
* **(Asterisk symbol)**	Used as a wildcard, for words that are unknown: eg *Microsoft acquires ***
related:	Finds websites that are similar to one you are familiar with: eg *related:bloomberg.com*
OR	Find pages that contain *one* of several words: eg *Plagiarism OR Malpractice*
site:	Returns results from specific URLs or domains: eg *site:bbc.co.uk, site:.com.cn*
info:	Finds cached versions of the site, related pages, or other pages that link to the site: eg *info:theguardian.com*
filetype:	Finds specific file types hosted online: eg *Leadership filetype:.ppt*

NOTE: The operators shown in this table will not work with every search engine. Also, this is not a complete list of operators, and there are many more out there. Have a look at the help section of your favourite search engine or try searching for 'search engine operators' to find ones that work for you.

Summary ✔

Trying to find evidence is a long and challenging task, with many students feeling as if they have found everything they can after only a few hours of searching. Unfortunately, research takes a long time and will require several attempts of trial and error. Sometimes ideas will lead you to a dead end, and other times you will encounter an endless list of resources. The key is to brainstorm and narrow down what you are looking for as early as possible, but also be willing to look into areas you may not have previously considered.

Keywords

Accuracy	The quality of being correct. Information provided is truthful and can be confirmed.
Authority	The quality of having influence and recognised knowledge about a topic.
Biased	In favour of or against something, usually in a way that is considered unfair or based on personal opinion.
Counter-argument	An idea or conclusion that is the opposite of the claim being made in what you are defending.
Currency	The quality of something being accepted or in use at this time.
Domains	Part of a network address, given at the end of a website URL.
Methodology	The approach or methods used when collecting research.
Objective	Providing ideas that are supported by evidence from different points of view. Not influenced by personal feelings or opinions.
Rebuttal	A statement given to disprove an idea. Used to disprove or highlight weaknesses in a counter-argument.
Subjective	Ideas influenced by personal feelings or opinions. Supported by little to no evidence.
Validity	The quality of being logical and reliable.

Introduction

While conducting your research, you will need to consider a few different things about every source you come across. Usually, published material such as books and journals have a high level of reliability compared to the average website found online. However, no matter where you collect your evidence from, you need to be very careful about what information you use. You need to be sure that the source is reliable and will support your paper in the best possible way.

Who? When? Where? Why?

Every time you come across a new source, there are some questions you must ask yourself. These questions should be asked of every source, including printed material (such as books and journals).

Who? (Authority)

» Who wrote the article? Are they experts?

» If it is a website, is the company or organisation reliable?

When? (Currency)

» When was the information written? Is it too old (outdated) for your topic?

» Is the source updated regularly? (*for digital media*)

Where? (Accuracy)

» Where did the source's evidence come from? Is there a reference list?

» Do you trust their information? Can you find and confirm the same details in other sources?

Why? (Objectivity)

» Why are they writing the article? To inform and educate, or to entertain?

» Are they **objective** or **subjective**? Are they trying to sell you something or persuade you?

Judging the reliability of websites

Generally, of all the different types of sources, websites cause the most difficulties when attempting to judge reliability. This is because the way to assess each site can vary depending on their purpose. This unit will cover a few examples, which will hopefully guide you in understanding the importance of judging reliability and how best to approach this task.

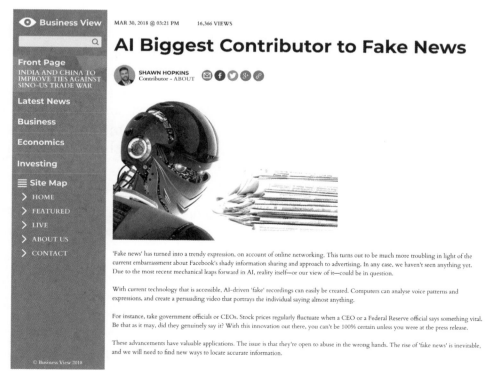

Judging authority (Who?)

The authority of a website is based on who wrote the article, or if no author is provided, then question which organisation or company hosts the site. On the previous page is an example of a source that clearly provides an author. You can quickly locate the name, Shawn Hopkins, below the title of the article. However, even if you have found the name of the author, you will still need to consider a few more points.

Essentially, you will need to decide if the author has any authority to discuss the topic in the article. As the primary focus in this example is artificial intelligence (AI), this author should have some experience either studying or working with the development of technologies in this field.

On most websites, if you click the author's name, you should be taken to a page that contains information about who they are. In this example, there is a link next to his name labelled 'About'. This will direct you to the following page.

SHAWN HOPKINS
Contributor

ABOUT   **RECENT POSTS**   CONTACT:

In 2012, Hopkins completed a PhD in Machine Learning at Massachusetts Institute of Technology (MIT). Since then, he has gone on to work for Google as the director of their AI Lab in Silicon Valley, California.

Hopkins has contributed heavily to the development of voice assistances, automated driving, and chipsets catered for deep learning methods.

As a regular contributor to Business View, Hopkins has provided detailed insights into the continuous developments in artificial intelligence and its impact on our future.

Beyond writing for Business View, Hopkins often appears at some of the most significant global tech events (such as CES, RE-WORK, and AI Expo Global). Furthermore, he often collaborates with many other big names in the industry to publish research papers in The Journal of Engineering and Technology Management (JET-M) and Technology in Society, to name a few.

From this page, it is clear to see this writer has the authority to discuss AI. He has studied a PhD relating to this field and has continued to research heavily in AI technologies, while also contributing to academic journals.

Furthermore, since graduating, he has several years' work experience with Google, a large tech company which is currently investing heavily in AI. This could lead to some **bias** in his writing, but this example article provides a balanced view on the subject, by both criticising and re-affirming AI's contributions.

NOTE: Not every website will have a link to an 'About' page like in this example. However, they may have sections called 'Profiles', or even 'About Us', where more details can be found about the writers or the organisation behind the website.

Whenever you locate an author's name, it would be a good idea to go to a search engine and find anything else they have written. In this example, Hopkins' 'About' page states that he has published journal articles. Therefore, searching for his published material should lead to more sources that are reliable and potentially useful in supporting your arguments.

If a website offers no authors in their articles, then you will need to look at the company or organisation that runs the website. Usually, there is a link to an 'About Us' section located somewhere on the site, and this will direct you to a page similar to the following one.

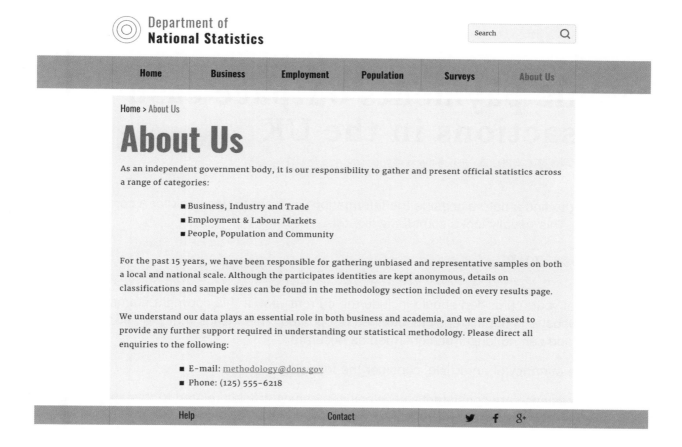

When analysing an 'About Us' page, pay attention to some of the following details.

» Look for independent bodies or non-profit organisations, as these usually provide objective information.

» Pay attention to how long they have been operating. The longer they have been around, the chances are they are a well-established group with a reputation to protect.

» Try to locate some contact details. A company or organisation that is willing to communicate is a bonus, and do not be afraid to get in touch if you have any questions about the information they have provided (perhaps you want to check their sources).

NOTE: The URL can also tell you a little bit about what organisation hosts the website. Look out for **domains** that are associated with academia (*.ac.uk*), non-profit organisations (*.org*), and government bodies (*.gov*).

Judging currency (When?)

It is important to know when the information was created and how often a website is updated. If a website is not updated often, then it could mean it's run by an individual and is unlikely to be their primary focus in life (possibly created as a hobby or out of personal interest in a subject).

Currency is usually the most straightforward piece of information to judge, as many websites provide you with a date of publication. Many sites also offer a time stamp on every single article they upload, and some even keep you updated on when a change or edit has occurred.

TECHinsider   Home ▽   Smartphones ▽   PC/Laptops ▽   Wearables ▽   🐦 f 8+ 𝓟 📷 Q

TODAY

Mobile payments outpace cash transactions in the UK

🕐 **18th March 2018 @ 4:23PM**   👤 **Judy Burgess** *@jburgesstechinsider* ↗

If you are struggling to find a date alongside the information you want to use, look for a copyright date at the bottom of the page. This usually looks something like this.

© *Techinsider 2005–2018*

The year (or range of years) provided should include the current year. If this copyright stamp is outdated, it indicates that the website is not currently maintained or updated. This means that the information provided may have changed and can no longer be confirmed as accurate.

When looking at the currency of an article, consider the following.

» Topics relating to science are consistently developing, meaning articles related to this subject need to be up to date. Try to find sources that have been published within the last few years.

» Concepts or studies into behaviours or patterns (in society or business environments) need to be judged for their appropriateness. Changes across generations may invalidate the articles, as their relevance no longer applies to current situations.

» When looking at research conducted by others, do not only pay attention to the date the article was written, but also identify when the data was collected.

Judging accuracy (Where?)

This may be the most challenging aspect of a source's reliability to judge. Mainly, you are trying to decide if you think the information is **valid**. If you are researching into a subject that is new to you, or if any of the information provided has a chance of being misrepresented, then you must examine the original source of the information.

There are two ways to check the accuracy and quality of information provided.

» Check for a reference list or links to the original source.

» Use the information you have collected and conduct another search.

This is a routine you should get familiar with, especially when dealing with statistical data. This kind of information can often be incorrectly interpreted across different websites, and it is your job to identify the correct numbers. Here are some steps you can follow when judging the accuracy and quality of a source that does not provide a reference list.

» **Make notes on the source** – write down what information you want to use as evidence and details of the source (eg *author, company/organisation, URL, date*).

» **Confirm information** – go to a search engine (or to your local library) and search using the information you have found. Look and see if the same details can be found elsewhere.

» **Compare** – look at the new sources you have located and compare the information. Look for similarities and differences.

» **Decide** – once you have decided the information is accurate, decide which source is the most reliable. It may be the first source you found, or it could be one of the new ones you have uncovered during the confirmation and comparison stages.

This process can be a little time-consuming, but as you do more research into your subject, you will become familiar with sources that are more reliable than others. This means that in the future, you will need to conduct less fact-checking and be comfortable in accepting the information provided to you by certain sources.

An example of this is to find the answer to the question: *'What was the GDP of Japan in 2016?'* Using a search engine and the keywords *'GDP Japan 2016'*, nearly 2 million results are returned. The website shown on page 96 is an example of one of these results.

The figure provided on this site is 4.940 trillion United States dollars (USD). Below the bar chart, this website clearly references two sources for this data: 'World Bank' and 'Economic and Social Research Institute'.

» The first source is a non-profit organisation that works closely with governments across 189 counties. Their main aim is to monitor the distribution of wealth across the globe, with a mission to eventually eliminate poverty.

» The second source is a department within the Cabinet Office, a section of the Japanese Government responsible for the collection of statistical data.

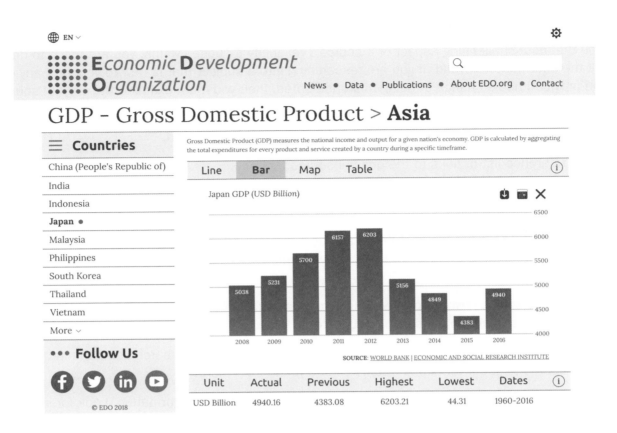

Unit	Actual	Previous	Highest	Lowest	Dates	ⓘ
USD Billion	4940.16	4383.08	6203.21	44.31	1960-2016	

Both of the sources mentioned could be considered as reliable for their collection of data. Furthermore, upon visiting each of the sources' websites, you can locate details of their **methodology**, allowing you to see exactly how the data was collected.

The website 'Economic Development Organisation' is also a non-profit organisation, which gathers data from a wide range of economic sources to promote the introduction of new polices that will serve to improve the lives of people from all over the world. Therefore, this website could be considered as accurate and authoritative.

Even if this website did not include any reference list, it would still be possible to consider this information as accurate. Looking at a few more of the results that were returned in the original search, the same figure can be located on many sites. Therefore, this confirms this data as accurate.

 NOTE: When looking to confirm statistical data, check the unit used. For example, GDP is often represented in USD, but sometimes it can be presented in a country's own currency. Furthermore, pay attention to the number itself, as it may be shown as 'millions' on one site, but then in 'billions' on another.

Judging objectivity (Why?)

There is always a reason behind why information has been written and published for all to see. There is always a purpose, whether it be to inform, entertain, educate or persuade. To understand the purpose, you need to think about the following information.

» **Author, company or organisation** – what is their involvement with this topic? Are they presenting this information to inform or educate you on changes and developments? Or will they benefit from persuading others to believe these ideas, such as a financial gain from selling a service or product?

» **Multiple points of view** – has the article provided different views on an idea? If there is an argument, have they then provided **counter-arguments** and **rebuttals**? Have they balanced the advantages and disadvantages fairly?

» **Language used throughout the article** – are they using any personal opinions or thoughts? Are there any emotions or feelings presented alongside their claim or towards the opposing argument?

» **Examine the page for advertisements** – if you locate a source with many advertisements, then can you trust their information to be unbiased? Is it possible that this website will present ideas to keep their advertisers happy?

Every example shown so far in this unit could be considered as objective, as they are written by reputable authors or organisations that want to inform and provide unbiased information. They all present ideas from different points of view, or they merely provide statistical data that has not been interpreted or repurposed into a particular claim. Finally, only the 'Techinsider' source contained advertisements, and this was limited to a single sidebar banner.

What to avoid?

So far, this unit has provided several examples of what to identify on a website to judge the source as reliable. However, it is also a good idea to look at a few examples of sources that would be considered unreliable.

Screen names

When looking for the author of an article, it is important to locate their real name. Some websites will only provide you with an online name, also known as a screen name. Sometimes for EAP students, it can be difficult to identify the names of people from different nationalities to their own. However, there are a few clues to help you identify screen names.

» **A single word** – if you are only provided with one word, this is usually a screen name. Even if it is a real name, such as *'Andrew'*, this does not allow you to do some research about this person. Other single word names may include multiple words presented with no spaces, such as *'SarahCaneUK'* or *'Coolguysimon'*.

» **Numbers, characters or symbols** – names that include numbers, a special character or symbol can also be identified as screen names. Some examples may be *'Frank_Smith14'* or *'ChenYing1993'*.

Without a real name, you cannot confirm if this author has the authority to write about this topic. This person could be a 12 year-old girl who is sat at home bored and has decided to create a website, or post something regarding a topic that she may be interested in but has no real education or experience.

Journalists (news articles)

Although some of the biggest news outlets do hire journalists that specialise in a specific subject, many journalists are assigned to write on a wide range of topics by their editor in chief. This means that these writers have to research and write about topics that they are unfamiliar with, and often on a tight deadline. This results in them often misinterpreting ideas or presenting incorrect data, often without referencing where they located this information.

Check who the journalist is that wrote the article you may be interested in using and locate what other articles they have written. If they are listed as a *'correspondent'*, *'senior reporter'*, or *'analyst'*, and have only written articles based on a single topic, then they may be somewhat reliable.

Karen Watts

Senior Technology Reporter for News Space

Recent Articles

☐ **Facebook granted third-party access to 87m user accounts**
⏰ *3rd April 2018*

☐ **Elon Musk targets Mars for future colonization**
⏰ *2nd April 2018*

☐ **Videos games once again linked to increase of gun violence**
⏰ *31st March 2018*

However, even if you think the reporter has some authority to discuss this topic, it would still be a good idea to check the accuracy of their information before using them as a source of evidence.

Question-and-answer websites

These websites should always be avoided when conducting research. They are not considered reliable for many reasons. First, there are no real names provided, and this means you cannot judge the authority of these authors. The people who answer the questions do not work for the company that hosts this website; they are members of the public who have signed up to try to 'help' other people.

Furthermore, most answers provide no reference to where they found the answer to these questions. Sometimes they might say a source name (eg an author, speaker, company or organisation), but rarely does anyone provide a link to the exact location of this information.

Just take a look at the example on the following page. You should be able to see some of these issues.

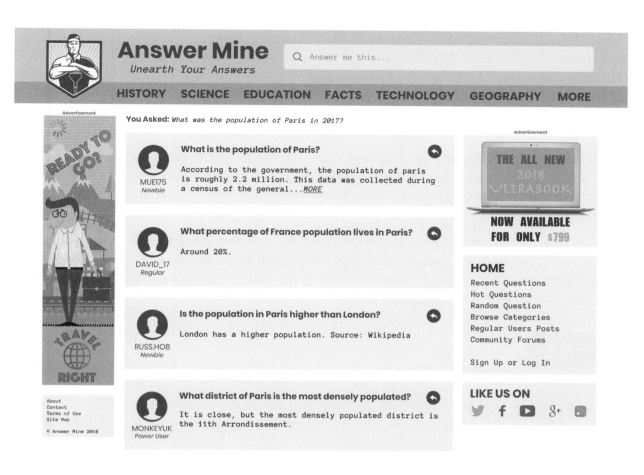

You Asked: *What was the population of Paris in 2017?*

What is the population of Paris?

MUE175
Newbie

According to the government, the population of paris is roughly 2.2 million. This data was collected during a census of the general...*MORE*

What percentage of France population lives in Paris?

DAVID_17
Regular

Around 20%.

Is the population in Paris higher than London?

RUSS.HOB
Newbie

London has a higher population. Source: Wikipedia

What district of Paris is the most densely populated?

MONKEYUK
Power User

It is close, but the most densely populated district is the 11th Arrondissement.

Finally, as you can see from the example above, these sites are heavily supported by advertisements. The teams that run these websites are made up of a small number of people, who rarely regulate the quality of the content published to the site. There is no large organisation that provides these services; they are simply created as a way to make money through advertisements.

Company websites and online shops

These sources provide biased information regarding their products and services. As the purpose of a company or store is to make money, they will only provide details that persuade the reader to buy something. They will focus on or highlight the benefits, but never provide any information regarding their disadvantages. Essentially, these kinds of sites are one big advertisement.

2018 Star Pro Desktop

Includes the **fastest** quad-core processor available on the market

Free from viruses (*unlike our competitors*)

Buy now and receive the worlds best word processing, spreadsheet, and slideshow editing software completely **free**!

BUY NOW: $ 1,999.00

Wikipedia and other wiki sites

Wiki websites, such as Wikipedia, have become a useful resource for most people in their daily lives. They offer an extensive collection of entries on a wide range of subjects and are often kept up to date. However, the information written on the page can be edited by anybody and presents similar problems to the question-and-answer sites. You cannot judge the authority of the author who has presented these details, which means you must look elsewhere to confirm the accuracy of the information provided.

Websites like Wikipedia can be useful as a starting point, a place for you to gather some background information relating to your topic. The entries will present you with keywords, respected figures, concepts, and even some relevant statistics. However, this information should then be used to conduct your research in other locations, either online or in the library.

A great place to look on a Wikipedia entry is the reference list provided at the bottom of each page. This will link you to any electronic sources that have been used while writing the article, or any books or journals that are related to the information covered throughout. Look at the sources provided, and if you judge these to be reliable, then you can use them in your paper. However, you cannot use Wikipedia as a source of evidence!

Summary ✔

Judging the reliability of any source takes practice, and all of the information covered in this unit can be used for any source you find, not just websites. Sometimes you will not be able to successfully judge the reliability of authority, currency, accuracy, and objectivity, but the more of these aspects that you can find relevant information about, the higher the source's quality will be in supporting your ideas.

It is crucial to ask questions and be critical about every piece of evidence you find. To successfully support your arguments, you need to gain an understanding of who has written the sources you locate during research, when and where they gathered their information, and why they have decided to write about this topic. Essentially, this skill requires you to use a high level of critical thinking.

Further reading

Although the examples provided in this unit are fictitious, they are based on the following websites. Spend some time examining and judging the reliability of these sites with the methods outlined in this unit.

Answers.com – www.answers.com [Answer Mine]

Apple – www.apple.com [Star Computers Store]

Forbes – www.forbes.com [Business View]

Office for National Statistics – www.ons.gov.uk [Department of National Statistics]

Organisation for Economic Co-operation and Development – www.oecd.org [Economic Development Organisation]

The Guardian – www.theguardian.com [News Space]

9to5mac – http://9to5mac.com [Tech Insider]

Unit 08
Reading techniques

8.1 – Reading comprehension

Keywords

Background reading	The reading of related articles or books to gain some contextual knowledge about your topic.
Critical thinking	The objective approach towards reaching a decision. Considering many points of view on a subject and making an informed decision.
Paraphrase	The presentation of others' ideas in your own words.
Reading strategy	An approach or method used to improve understanding while reading.
Reliability	The quality of being trustworthy and accurate.

Introduction

While researching for an academic paper, students often find understanding the sources they have found to be a challenge, especially if the topic is relatively new to them. As many reliable sources are written in academic or technical language, this makes the task of reading even more complicated, especially for EAP students. It is important to ask yourself some questions while reading a source.

» Do you understand the majority of what you read?

» Do you monitor how much you understand in each section?

» Are you able to understand the material you find uninteresting?

» Do you have any strategies for understanding more?

Reading strategies

It is important to approach any reading task with a strategy in mind. This varies depending on the purpose of the reading, and may even be influenced by the topic, how much time you have, or even the type of language used. Here are a few suggested approaches that will aid in your understanding.

Background reading

If you do not understand a source due to its topic, then go and read a more accessible text first. For EAP students, possibly read about the topic in your native language. This should help you understand the context of the topic and introduce you to some of the associated keywords or phrases that will not only help you understand the more challenging texts but will also aid in widening your searches.

Take notes

Monitor your understanding by writing a summary of each paragraph. Read an entire paragraph first, or if the paragraph is very long, then read a few sentences and stop. Without looking back at the text, write a summary. Once you have finished reading the source, this will allow you to quickly review the ideas and check for any gaps in your understanding.

Have a reading aim

Before you start reading, give yourself an aim. For example, this could be a list of questions you hope to answer. You can add to this list as you read the source, because you may uncover new ideas that were not thought of during the brainstorming stage. Knowing what you are looking for will help focus your attention, especially when reading difficult or uninteresting sources.

Re-read difficult sections

Academic sources, such as journals, are challenging to read. Even many native English speakers will have difficulties in understanding some paragraphs. Do not panic, and do not give up because you think it is too complicated. Re-read the paragraph slowly and several times until you begin to take in the general meaning. You do not need to understand every word; it is the context that is more important to grasp.

Highlight keywords and phrases

In your paper, you are going to be using some of the same keywords or phrases found in the sources that you have collected. Therefore, you should be highlighting them as you read and writing them in your notes. Even when **paraphrasing**, you will be using the same keywords that are commonly related to the topic. However, be careful; don't highlight everything, as this will make it hard for you to identify the most useful information.

Use critical thinking

Use your critical thinking skills to identify the purpose of the source.

» What is the author trying to prove? What is their main point?

» Why is this detail relevant? What is the purpose of this sentence/paragraph?

» Is the author trying to answer a particular question?

» What can I learn from this source?

Feel relaxed

It is much easier to understand something when you feel relaxed. Therefore, try to read in a pleasant environment with few distractions. Use a room with suitable lighting, some music or silence (depending on which works better for you), and drink plenty of water. Furthermore, make sure you are well rested and do not try to read too much in one day.

Translating

For EAP students, it is very common to want to translate every word in a sentence. This is not a good way to read and understand a piece of writing. Do not translate every word! The best piece of advice for you is to read the sentence and understand the context first. Once you understand the context, then you will be able to guess what many of the more difficult words mean.

If the entire sentence is a string of complicated words, then only translate a few words. Do not translate every word as this is a waste of your time. You should not copy the author's words into your essay, so you do not need to know every word's definition. By understanding the meaning behind the sentence, you can then paraphrase the idea into your own words.

Summary ✓

The task of reading can divide a group; many people love reading, while others find it challenging. Regardless of which side you fall on, the ability to understand what you read can be improved by the approach you take. Do not open up a source and start reading without some strategies in place. Create an aim based on what you want to get from the source, ask critical questions, take notes, and focus on what the source is telling you and not the words they have used. Once you have an understanding of the source, then you can review and judge the language for other reasons, such as the **reliability** of the evidence.

8.2 – Skimming and scanning

Keywords

Cohesive device	Used in essays to link paragraphs (or sentences) together.
Concluding sentence	Used to signal that the current idea has been explored in sufficient detail.
Essay map	A cohesive device that presents a summary of the main body's controlling ideas.
Preview	To take a quick look at something and gather a few basic ideas before revisiting in detail.
Thesis statement	A sentence provided in the introduction paragraph. This will outline the main claim of the entire essay.
Topic sentence	A sentence given at the start of each main body paragraph to express the main idea that will be explored within it.

Introduction

Taking care to understand the information you find in your research is essential, but it is also beneficial for your time management if you can improve your reading speed. Depending on what you are hoping to find in a source, there are different methods of reading you can attempt.

Skimming

The purpose of skimming a text is to find the general meaning and ideas within it. This allows you to decide if the source is related to the ideas you want to cover in your essay. It can be very annoying and time-consuming if you read an entire text in detail, only to then discover it is not useful in any way. Therefore, it is recommended that you **preview** a text first using the following method.

» Read the title.

» Read any headings or subheadings.

» Read the introduction and/or the first paragraph.

» Read the conclusion and/or the final paragraph.

» Read the first and last sentence of every paragraph.

» Notice any pictures, graphs, charts, tables, etc.

» Notice any *italicised* or **boldface** words (these are often keywords/phrases).

You will notice that some of the areas listed above rely on the use of **cohesive devices**. You are attempting to identify **thesis statements**, **essay maps**, **topic sentences**, and **concluding sentences**. This demonstrates the importance of including these elements in your paper, as they are useful for your reader should they wish to preview (or review) your essay.

Scanning

Scanning is used when you have a clear aim in mind, as the purpose is to find a specific piece of information. This technique is useful for locating information such as a name, number, date, or location. Essentially, you need to move your eyes around the page very quickly until you locate the desired information. Activities such as word searches give you an excellent opportunity to practise the skill of scanning on a smaller scale. Have a go at the *Academic Writing Word Search* below.

```
X  I  U  K  O  Q  R  E  F  E  R  E  N  C  I  N  G  A  T  E
K  N  R  E  S  E  A  R  C  H  G  Q  A  A  Q  W  O  B  W  I
J  K  L  Z  F  N  T  H  E  S  I  S  J  E  H  R  I  H  G  Y
E  K  X  O  E  B  T  P  S  C  A  N  N  I  N  G  G  F  B  Y
P  A  P  Z  K  C  T  A  O  J  B  N  P  X  S  O  W  K  Y  S
H  B  W  Y  B  Q  R  R  P  T  E  A  A  R  S  S  F  T  Z  X
Q  B  N  B  R  E  F  A  N  A  Z  N  R  K  M  K  I  G  N  D
D  Y  X  Z  L  R  H  P  D  H  O  M  A  Z  Q  L  S  O  I  R
M  J  A  J  Y  B  M  H  X  I  F  M  G  Z  I  X  K  T  M  A
C  K  P  L  S  Z  Y  R  T  I  B  Y  R  B  N  C  I  W  Y  B
O  H  R  H  L  R  K  A  D  D  C  S  A  P  T  A  M  R  L  B
N  W  O  S  A  R  T  S  A  M  J  I  P  A  R  I  M  A  I  U
C  B  X  M  E  O  C  I  H  Y  L  Y  H  J  O  L  I  H  T  G
L  I  M  E  U  Y  K  N  T  E  Z  G  C  Q  D  D  N  F  E  R
U  U  T  Q  E  U  X  G  R  C  F  D  O  J  U  R  G  M  S  I
S  X  I  A  E  V  I  D  E  N  C  E  H  R  C  H  Y  Z  M  R
I  E  J  T  T  V  E  P  M  G  M  U  Z  I  T  K  V  T  Q  A
O  L  E  Z  H  I  O  O  X  S  Y  J  R  D  I  E  G  F  V  L
N  I  R  T  Z  Y  O  S  Y  M  U  P  Y  A  O  K  I  Q  W  Z
M  F  H  P  L  Z  R  N  X  W  H  J  C  V  N  A  R  D  O  B
```

Citation	Conclusion	Evidence	Introduction	Paragraph	Paraphrasing	Quotation
Referencing	Reliability	Research	Scanning	Skimming	Summary	Thesis

Summary ✔

Although understanding your sources is essential, the methods presented in this unit are there to save you time while reading. These reading skills are useful when you are starting out with research, as you will often have to work your way through many different sources before you find the most relevant pieces of evidence. Once you have located the sources that provide you with information that is supportive of your claims, you can go back over the important sections in detail.

8.3 – SQ3R

Keywords

Assessment task	Details of what you are expected to do in your assignment. Could be provided in the form of a question.
Record	To take notes on something.
Review	To look back at something, to check for details or refresh your memory.
Survey	To take a quick look at something and gather a few basic ideas before revisiting in detail.
Symbol	A mark or character that carries meaning, used to represent something else.

Introduction

The methods of reading in the previous unit are useful for saving time while initially locating information, or during a quick review of a text that you are somewhat familiar with. However, perhaps your tutor has supplied you with an article that you will need to use in your paper, or you want to read something in a little more detail and record the relevant information. In these situations, there is another method you can use to comprehend the ideas presented throughout a source.

SQ3R

This method is considered to be one of the most effective and efficient approaches to reading challenging texts. It was originally proposed by Francis P. Robinson, a philosopher in education, during the 1960s. He suggested this approach for college students who struggled to comprehend their textbooks. This has been widely adopted and is still relevant today when attempting to read any problematic source material.

This method requires you to follow a series of steps that take place before, during, and after reading; *Survey, Question, Read, Record,* and *Review*.

Survey

This stage requires you to use the skimming technique covered in the previous unit. Focus your attention towards these specific areas of the source to identify its purpose.

» Read the title, headings or subheadings.

» Read the introduction/first paragraph and conclusion/final paragraph.

» Read the captions below any pictures, graphs, charts and tables.

Furthermore, review the details provided in the **assessment task** and your essay (if you have started writing; otherwise, look at your outline and any brainstorming notes you have created). Refresh your memory on what it is you need to find to support your claims.

Question

Next, you will need to create questions based on the surveying stage. Use the details collected from looking at the title, headings, subheadings, introduction, conclusion, and any captions you have read. Additionally, create questions based on what details are needed to help support your claims. This information should give you an idea of what it is you are expecting to read in the main text.

Read

As you read, think about the questions you have created. Have any of these questions been answered? If so, highlight or underline these areas. Furthermore, you may also want to highlight any keywords or phrases that are going to be useful in your paper, or in future searches.

Take the time to look at any visual aids, such as pictures, graphs or charts. These can help you to understand some of the ideas covered in the main text.

If you find certain sections of the source to be difficult, slow down and review them. Try not to read the entire source in one attempt; break it up into sections (one or two paragraphs at a time). After each section, make some notes (see the next stage).

Record

As you read each section of a source, take the time to write some notes. Write a summary of what each section covers: its main ideas, any claims it makes, any data or statistics presented, or other important details (eg names, locations and dates). However, write these notes in your own words. Do not copy out sentences into your notes, as this may lead to you copying them directly into your paper.

Review

Finally, review your questions and your essay (or outline/brainstorm). Try to identify which of these questions can be answered, or if any claims can be supported by the information in your notes. You can save this review stage until the very end of the source, or you can do this step after each section.

Do not waste time going back to look for answers in the source, as you should have noted all the crucial details in your notes. If you cannot find the information, then you will need to continue your research elsewhere.

Abbreviations and symbols

The use of abbreviations and symbols can be useful when note-taking, to write down information quickly and concisely. Over the page is a table of some potential symbols and abbreviations you could use. However, your notes are personal, which means you can use any symbols and abbreviations you want as long as you understand their meaning.

Symbol/abbreviation	Meaning	Symbol/abbreviation	Meaning
&	And	≠	Not the same
+	Plus/in addition/and	w/	With
<	Less than	>	More than/leads to
=	The same/equal to	e.g.	For example
i.e.	That means	etc.	And the rest/plus more
NB	Important/notice this	wd	Would
p	Page number	Govt.	Government
Para	Paragraph	Edu	Education
Ch	Chapter	impt	Important
Ed	Edition	info	Information
cd	Could	ASAP	As soon as possible

Summary ✔

Throughout this set of units, there have been many suggestions regarding the approaches to reading. This unit presents the SQ3R method, which highlights the importance of two essential techniques: have a reading aim, and taking notes. By using this method, you will be able to improve your comprehension through focusing your attention towards the relevant information and by monitoring your understanding. The process of note-taking is a crucial factor in how you will use sources in your essay, which is the focus of the next unit.

Further reading

For more details about SQ3R, check out the following resource:

Robinson, F. P. (1978) *Effective Study*. 6th edn. New York: Harper & Row.

Unit 09
Using others' ideas

9.1 – Preparation

Keywords

Critical reading	An approach to reading that requires you to ask questions and think carefully about the quality of the information presented.
Paraphrase	The presentation of others' ideas in your own words.
Referencing	The act of providing details that inform the reader where your evidence has been used and where the original text can be found.
Skimming	To take a quick look at something and gather a few basic ideas before revisiting in detail.
SQ3R	A reading strategy that requires you to preview the text, formulate questions, read and make notes, and then review to monitor your understanding (see Unit 8.3).
Survey	To take a quick look at something and gather a few basic ideas before revisiting in detail.

Introduction

Before presenting any evidence, you will need to spend a little time preparing what information you plan to provide in your essay. Additionally, to effectively support your claims, and provide evidence as **paraphrases** or **summaries**, a deep understanding of the details in each source is essential.

Critical reading

Based on the reading techniques covered in the previous set of units, you should have a rough idea of a source's content before you begin to read it in detail (via the use of **skimming** or **surveying** the text). At this stage, you will then need to read and re-read the relevant sections that relate to the claim you are trying to make. The **SQ3R** method is especially useful for monitoring your understanding while reading.

To read critically, you need to be consistently asking questions of each section. Below are just some of the questions you should be asking.

» What is the argument or claim this author is trying to convey to the reader?

» Whom is this source aimed at? Who is the target audience?

» What do I already know about this topic? Have I read similar sources before?

» What have I learnt from reading this source? What information is new and interesting to me?

Remember, if you are unfamiliar with a topic, do some background reading. Locate a source that is easier for you to understand and gain some basic knowledge about this subject. Having some background knowledge of the topic, including a grasp of related keywords, will certainly help with your understanding of more challenging sources.

Note-taking

It is essential that you make notes whenever you are reading a source that you intend to use in your paper. Do not just read a source, decide you are happy with it, and then start writing it into your essay. Highlight the sections/paragraphs you find the most useful, pick up your pen and make notes about your understanding, and be sure to use your own words (except for key words and phrases).

Think about some of the following questions while making notes.

» Do you actually need this information? If so, which parts?

» Will you really use it? When, and how?

» Have you noticed similar information already?

» What claims do you want to support with this information?

Remember to keep your notes brief. Try writing down the main ideas, then put your pen down and continue reading. If you keep your pen in your hand the whole time, you will be tempted to write more than you need.

 NOTE: Also, take note of where you found the source. This information is required for **referencing**, and it will also help you find the source again at a later date. For example, if it is a book, write down the author, title of the book, edition, and publisher details (see Unit 10 for more details on referencing).

The following is an extract taken from an article entitled 'Meeting the Needs of Chinese Students in British Higher Education'. These few sentences discuss the topic of academic plagiarism.

* Example

'While plagiarism is by no means a recent phenomenon, the rapid growth in international students may well have served as a catalyst for current discussions. In the West, the author is considered to be the sole creator of the text; plagiarism is perceived by some as a violation of the author and is considered to be morally wrong' (Edwards and An, 2006).

For EAP students, there are plenty of difficult words contained in this extract. However, you do not need to understand every word to comprehend the idea being presented.

The first half of the sentence may confuse some students, as it uses the phrase 'is by no means', which essentially means 'is not', and the word 'phenomenon', which is probably new vocabulary for most. However, you can ignore this part, as the second half of this sentence is where the central claim is being made.

> '...the rapid growth in international students may well have served as a catalyst for current discussions' (Edwards and An, 2006).

The statement 'growth in international students' means there are now more students studying from overseas. The rest of the sentence contains a few difficult phrases/words, such as 'catalyst', but you can ignore these and still gain an understanding of the context. It then ends by saying 'current discussions'; you know the topic of this article is 'plagiarism', so you can assume that plagiarism is the topic that is being discussed currently.

At this stage, your notes may look something like this.

Meeting the needs of Chinese students in British higher education - Viv Edwards and An Ran

Claim: more students from overseas has caused more discussions relating to plagiarism.

Questions: because? Maybe they don't understand what plagiarism is? Maybe copying from an author is encouraged in their home country?

Notice how the notes include some questions, as this section of the source does not provide a reason why more overseas students have caused an increase in concern regarding this topic. Questions like this help focus your attention as you read the rest of the article, and if this question is not answered by this source, then finding the answer to these questions will be helpful as you continue to research.

Now, taking a look at the next sentence, some sections that EAP students may find difficult to understand have been crossed out.

> 'In the West, the author is ~~considered to be~~ the ~~sole~~ creator of the text; plagiarism is ~~perceived by some as a violation of the author and is considered to be morally~~ wrong' (Edwards and An, 2006).

Maybe some of the crossed-out sections can be understood by a few students, but even someone with a basic grasp of the English language should be able to understand that the text above is essentially saying.

Claim:

- In places like the UK or US, the writer is the owner of their words.

- Plagiarism is wrong! It is a form of cheating / stealing.

Now, you have a collection of ideas taken from the source. From these points, the claims can be understood and presented in the following form.

> *According to Edwards and An (2006), plagiarism has recently become a more common topic of discussion in education, mainly due to an increased number of overseas students. This act of directly copying others' words is seen as a form of stealing in Western countries (Edwards and An, 2006).*

The sentences above express the main ideas being presented by the source. This new collection of sentences is known as a paraphrase, which will be covered in more detail in the next unit.

Summary ✔

To use a source correctly in your paper, you will need to spend a little time understanding and making notes about the source's details before writing anything. For a source to sufficiently support your argument, you need to decide if is relevant, what content will be required, and how to use it in your paper. Taking the time to make notes will help monitor your understanding and allow you to produce paraphrases or summaries that convey the correct meaning and avoid the potential risk of plagiarism.

References

Edwards, V. and An, R. (2006) *Meeting the Needs of Chinese Students in British Higher Education*. Available at: https://blogs.shu.ac.uk/internationalnetwork/files/2013/07/MeetingTheNeeds.pdf (Accessed: 7 April 2018).

9.2 – Paraphrasing

Keywords

Academic misconduct	A term used to describe cheating in education, such as stealing other people's words or ideas.
Citation	Provided whenever evidence has been used in an essay. Part of the referencing process.
Clarity	The quality of being clear and easily understood.
Paraphrase	The presentation of others' ideas in your own words.
Reference list	Given at the end of an essay. Provides further details that are not given alongside the citation (eg book title, website URL).
Synonym	Words or phrases that have the same meaning.

Introduction

In academic writing, when using the ideas of others, you are expected to present your understanding and interpretation of their claims. If you just copy the words of others, you are not doing anything unique with this information. Therefore, you should use your own words as much as possible throughout your paper.

Why paraphrase?

There are many reasons why you should paraphrase the words of others when presenting their ideas in your paper. Here are three reasons to consider.

» **Give clarity** – the evidence you have read will often be very academic, professional, and somewhat difficult for some readers to understand. You have spent a long time researching and understanding your topic, but your reader may not have the same experience. Therefore, expressing ideas in your own words should help simplify the information and make it more accessible to your readers.

» **Show understanding** – simply copying the words of others does not show that you have understood your topic. It just shows you can find information, which is no more impressive than a list of search engine results. If you present the research in your own words, it shows you have taken the time to read and understand the ideas carefully.

» **Avoid plagiarism** – if you copy the words of others, there is always a risk of someone classifying it as plagiarism. Copying the words of others is seen as a form of cheating by universities and will result in your paper scoring zero.

Referencing

Whenever you use the ideas of others (not just their words), you need to show where you found this information. Therefore, when paraphrasing, you need to provide something called a **citation** and an entry in your **reference list**. The citation can be given as part of the sentence (if you refer to the author's name directly), or it can go at the very end of the sentence. More details on how to correctly reference can be found in Unit 10.

NOTE: Even though the words are your own, a paraphrase still contains somebody else's idea. Not giving a citation AND an entry in the reference list is a form of **academic misconduct** (poor referencing/plagiarism). Cases of misconduct will result in a penalty.

How to paraphrase?

Paraphrasing can be broken down into a five-step process.

» **Critically read and understand your source** – first, you need to locate the evidence you wish to use in your paper. Read the text and grasp an understanding of the meaning; specifically, what idea or claim is the writer trying to express?

» **Take notes** – as the example in the previous unit showed you, it is important to make notes about the meaning of each sentence. Remember to keep them brief and write these in your own words, only copying over the keywords.

» **Write out your understanding (based on your notes)** – do not look at the source; only look at your notes. Write down the idea/claim using your own words, being sure to use full sentences (not just brief statements from your notes).

» **Check your paraphrase** – read your paraphrase. Does it make sense? Is it clear? Look back at the original source; check and see if they look the same. If they look similar, then try again! You should make your paraphrase look different from the original while still keeping the same meaning.

» **Provide a reference** – if you have not already done so in your paraphrase, make sure you provide a citation. At the same time, go down to your reference list and write in an entry for this source. Do not leave it until you have finished writing your paper, as you may forget to include it!

Checking your paraphrase

Sometimes it is quite challenging to check your paraphrases, as you may feel you have made sufficient changes. However, there are a few options available for you to have your work checked.

» **Arrange a tutorial** – or at the very least, send an email to your tutor. However, be very specific which areas of your essay need attention. If you ask a tutor to check your entire draft, they may overlook some poor attempts at paraphrasing. However, if you ask them to check certain sentences or paragraphs, they are more likely to provide targeted feedback on your paraphrases.

English for Academic Purposes: A Handbook for Students

- » **Plagiarism checkers** – there are a few services available online, such as Turnitin, that check your work for cases of plagiarism that may have occurred due to poor paraphrasing. Many of these services are not free to everyone, but most universities provide free access via their student websites (ie Moodle or Blackboard).
- » **Search engine (self-check)** – this last option is available to everyone with an internet connection. Copy your paraphrase, paste it into a search engine, and if the source appears at the top of the results with many boldfaced words, then you have not sufficiently paraphrased the text.

Search engine (self-check) example

Using the same extract from the previous unit, here is an example of a poor paraphrase.

> *In the UK, the author is thought to be the writer of the text; plagiarism is seen by some as a violation of the writer and is seen to be wrong. Plagiarism is not a recent problem; the fast increase in international students may well have served as a reason for current talks (Edwards and An, 2006).*

Several words have been changed, and the sentences have been switched. However, it is still very similar to the original. It is so similar that if you put these two sentences into a search engine (without the authors' names), it would be able to easily find the original text.

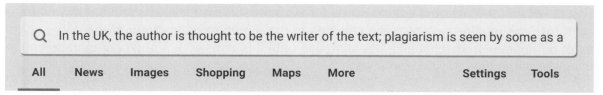

About 390,000 results (1.70 seconds)

[PDF] **Meeting the needs of Chinese students in British Higher... - SHU Blogs**
https://blogs.shu.ac.uk/internationalnetwork/files/2013/07/MeetingTheNeeds.pdf ⌄
by V Edwards - 2006 - Cited by 58 - Related articles
reports. While report and essay **writing** appear to **cause** fewer **problems**, critical analysis and **problem** solving are often identified as areas of weakness. Oral presentation was another area for concern. **Plagiarism**. In the west, **plagiarism** is perceived by **some** as a **violation** of the **author** and is **considered** to be morally **wrong**.

The source this paraphrase was based on appeared in the top few results. As you can see, several matching words have been highlighted in bold, some of which cannot be changed (eg the keyword '*plagiarism*'). However, the other words could easily be changed for **synonyms**.

NOTE: In some cases, no matter how much you change, you will sometimes get the original source back in the results. However, this is usually due to specific keywords, or pieces of data that can only be found on a select few websites. If this is the case, have your paraphrase checked by your tutor.

If you can locate the source easily, then it means your paraphrase is too similar to the original. Your tutor will be able to locate it just as quickly, and you will then be accused of poor academic practice or possibly even plagiarism.

What to keep?

As this unit has already covered, you should be writing out the ideas or claims in your own words. However, there will be some elements of the original that you have to keep the same. Here is a list of what counts as keywords that can be kept in your paraphrases.

» **Names/locations** – nouns, such as names or places that are given in the original source, and are essential to the idea you are paraphrasing, will need to remain the same.

» **Subject/topic vocabulary** – words that are related to the topic you are writing about. For example, the word *plagiarism* will be required when talking about academic misconduct, as this keyword often appears in texts referring to this topic.

» **Data/numbers/statistics** – percentages, financial figures (costs), years, or any other form of numerical data will need to be kept the same. Unless you are interpreting visual data, then you may need to avoid referring to the actual number but focus more on the differences or changes.

Changing the structure

Paraphrasing is not just the act of changing words for synonyms; it also involves presenting ideas in an entirely new form. This requires you to make changes to the structure or grammar of the entire sentence. Try not to think of paraphrasing as 'changing the sentence until it is different'. A good paraphrase should focus on expressing the same idea in your own style.

Look at the structure of the original text and identify how the information is provided. While making notes about the claim and any keywords, also write down a few points about the order in which information is presented. This should help you construct a paraphrase that provides details in a new form.

 NOTE: Although not a rule/academic feature followed by every university (or even by every tutor within a university), students are sometimes asked to avoid the passive form in academic writing. Therefore, try to keep the passive form to a minimum or, if possible, attempt to remove the subject while paraphrasing.

As an example, if the sentence states a particular situation and then what happened because of this (*cause then effect*), try presenting the information in the opposite order during your paraphrase (*effect then cause*). Take a look at the sentences below.

> *Original (cause > effect): The extensive use of fossil fuels over the past 50 years has resulted in an increased atmospheric temperature and rising sea levels.*
>
> *Paraphrase (effect > cause): Global warming and the rise in sea levels are a result of half a century of overreliance on fossil fuels.*

Another example would be to switch an idea that is presented as an active statement into a passive form. Alternatively, if the subject is unnecessary, or easily identified, then you can simply remove it from the sentence. Take a look at the following examples.

Original (active): *Scientists in the US have discovered proof that smoking does increase the risk of lung cancer.*

Paraphrase 1 (passive): *Evidence that proves cases of lung cancer are more common among smokers has been uncovered by US scientists.*

Paraphrase 2 (remove the subject): *Recent findings demonstrate that smokers have a much higher chance of being diagnosed with lung cancer.*

Summary ✔

The idea of paraphrasing sounds quite simple, but the ability to produce high-quality paraphrases does take time. This skill does rely heavily on you understanding the idea being presented by the source, as without this understanding you will be tempted to copy as much as possible to ensure the correct meaning is provided.

Note-taking is essential and should aid in the creation of an original paraphrase. By using brief statements, written in your own words, you should be able to create something that is visually different from the original. However, do not forget to go back and check the actual meaning has been retained. Sometimes essential information is removed, or extra details are added, resulting in a paraphrase that misrepresents the original idea. Avoid this mistake by spending that little extra time checking your paraphrase is accurate.

References

Edwards, V. and An, R. (2006) *Meeting the Needs of Chinese Students in British Higher Education*. Available at: https://blogs.shu.ac.uk/internationalnetwork/files/2013/07/MeetingTheNeeds.pdf (Accessed: 2018).

Keywords

Academic misconduct	A term used to describe cheating in education, such as stealing other people's words or ideas.
Citation	Provided whenever evidence has been used in an essay. Part of the referencing process.
Coherent	The quality of being logical and consistent. Ideas are linked together and easy to follow.
Discussion	Used to analyse evidence and highlight the connection between your idea and what is stated in the evidence.
Paraphrase	The presentation of others' ideas in your own words.
Reference list	Given at the end of an essay. Provides further details that are not given alongside the citation (eg book title, website URL).
Supporting point	A statement that is provided in your main body paragraphs. This supports the claim and controlling idea provided in the topic sentence.

Introduction

Summarising is very similar to **paraphrasing**. The critical difference is that summarising is used to express many ideas, or a very long and complex idea, into a few sentences. The steps to complete a summary are very similar to those used in creating a paraphrase, resulting in the idea being presented in your own words.

How to summarise

As mentioned previously, the required steps in writing a summary are essentially the same as a paraphrase.

» **Read and critically analyse the source material** – for a paraphrase, this is usually just a sentence or two. However, a summary could include ideas from several paragraphs (or possibly ideas presented across the entire source).

» **Take notes** – this is especially important as you are pulling together numerous details. Jumping between ideas on a page will confuse you, and result in an unclear summary that has possibly left out key details. Furthermore, note-taking will help you avoid cases of plagiarism.

» **Write a summary of your notes** – do not look back at the original. Again, this is done to avoid copying chunks of text (*plagiarism*).

» **Check your summary against the original** – Use a search engine, just like with the paraphrasing example in the previous unit. If they are similar, make more changes. Be sure the summary is written in your words, using your own style.

» **Do not forget to reference** – Provide a **citation** in, or after, the summary; and do not forget to write an entry in your **reference list** at the end of the paper.

 NOTE: Even though a summary is your own words, just like paraphrases, the ideas are taken from somebody else. Therefore, references must be given, or you risk being accused of **academic misconduct**, and your work will score zero.

Read through the following article about plagiarism in China.

---

* Example

In China, it is extremely common for students to copy the words of others, possibly because this practice is often taught at high schools across the country. However, this becomes an issue when these students apply to study overseas as they will often submit papers with large extracts of text taken from books and websites.

On the Sino-British collaborative programmes in Chengdu, students are often caught plagiarising the words of others. In many cases, the students believe the information they provided did not require references, as they feel these details are known by all and are essentially examples of common knowledge.

Cases like these suggest that students do not grasp the idea that the original author is the owner of these words, and that copying what they have written is actually a form of stealing. They believe their actions to be acceptable and not a form of cheating.

The internet and other digital resources have made the act of plagiarism a much more manageable task for students to undertake. Because information is so readily available, and other forms of 'sharing' (such as music and video torrents) are familiar to these students, there appears to be a severe lack of understanding of the concept of authorship.

Author: Drew Graham   *Date: 10 April 2018*

The next step is to make notes about what information could be useful in a summary of this text. Following is an example of some possible notes.

Plagiarism in China - Drew Graham (2018)

- Students do not realise what they are doing is wrong
  > High school taught them differently.
- The internet makes it easier to access information.
- This generation is familiar with illegally sharing files online
  > Showing a lack of understanding or care of ownership.

From these notes, you can see there are three main ideas presented across the four paragraphs. Using these three ideas, a summary could be written as follows.

> *Graham (2018) suggests that most Chinese students commit plagiarism due to a lack of understanding surrounding rules of ownership. He adds that this could be a result of the high school education system encouraging the use of others' words in their writing, and possibly that growing up in a digital age has conditioned them to be comfortable with the act of illegally sharing copyrighted material (Graham, 2018).*

Finally, comparing this summary to the original article, there are very few words or phrases repeated. The ideas that were noted down have been expressed in the summary above but have now taken on a new form.

 NOTE: The first sentence provides an 'in-text citation', and another is presented at the end of the second sentence. This is done to identify that both sentences are evidence and not part of your **supporting point** or **discussion**. More details on referencing can be found in Unit 10.

Summary ✔

Essentially, the process of creating and checking a summary is the same as paraphrasing. The crucial difference is the first step, which relates to where the ideas are sourced. Paraphrasing focuses on a small extract of text, usually one or two sentences. However, a summary is used to gather ideas from across a source. This should not cause too many difficulties, but do pay attention to how the ideas are presented and make sure they are still **coherent** in your summary.

9.4 – Translations

Keywords

Academic misconduct	A term used to describe cheating in education, such as stealing other people's words or ideas.
Citation	Provided whenever evidence has been used in an essay. Part of the referencing process.
Paraphrase	The presentation of others' ideas in your own words.
Reference list	Given at the end of an essay. Provides further details that are not given alongside the citation (eg book title, website URL).

Introduction

For EAP students, researching in their native language is often the easiest way to locate evidence. However, tutors will strongly recommend that you use English. However, this may not always be possible, especially when writing about topics that relate to your native country. Therefore, when using sources written in your native language, you will need to translate the information correctly.

Machine and direct translations

The important thing to remember is that you need to use your own words throughout your paper. This includes words that have been translated from your native language. Using a machine to translate sentences, or even paragraphs, is not considered to be your own words.

For your tutors, it is often quite clear when machine translation has been used. As they read the paper, they will notice a change in writing style, as the grammar begins to resemble that of your native language. Furthermore, machine translations tend to present vocabulary that is uncommon, and unlikely to be known by the students.

Even if you do not use a machine to translate entire sentences, changing one word at a time from your native language into English is still unacceptable and is known as a direct translation. This is still a form of copying, and therefore regarded as **academic misconduct**.

Detecting poor translations

If machine or direct translation has been used, it is very easy for the tutor to translate sections back into the student's native language and use a search engine to check for similarities with the original source. Here is an example that one Chinese student included in their essay.

> *The European Union is not only the British largest export destination (accounting for 46.9% of the total UK exports) but also the British largest source of imports destination (accounting for 52.3% of total UK imports). More than 60% of Euro transactions and more than 40% of global dollar transactions are completed in London, withdrew from the EU, Britain most cross-border financial institutions may transfer from London, large-scale Euro transactions may not be allowed, then London financial centre position may not protect.*

Upon reading these few sentences, it was clear that the language was different from the rest of the paper. There were noticeable errors in sentence structure that are similar to the way in which ideas are presented in the Chinese language. Therefore, this extract was translated into Chinese using translation software.

欧盟不仅是英国最大的出口目的地（占英国出口总额的46.9%），也是英国最大的进口目的地（占英国进口总额的52.3%）。超过60%欧元的交易和全球超过百分之40美元的交易是在伦敦完成的，从欧盟退出，英国大多数跨国金融机构可能从伦敦转移，大规模的欧元交易可能不被允许，那么伦敦金融中心的地位可能不保。

As you will notice, this student did not include any **citations** (or even a **reference list** entry). Therefore, this is already considered to be case of plagiarism, but the source still needs to be located. Therefore, using Baidu (the most popular search engine in China), this translation was located on the following website.

对英国来说，欧盟是英国最重要的贸易伙伴，退出欧盟之后，英国与欧盟的贸易模式将面临重构，对外贸易将受到冲击。由于欧盟区域内实行零关税政策，各国之间的贸易关系十分密切。据统计，<u>欧盟不仅是英国的第一大出口目的经济体（占英国出口总额的46.9%），也是英国第一大进口来源经济体(占英国进口总额的52.3%)</u>。此外，加入欧盟后，英国有超过百分之五十的新增服务贸易来自欧盟，退出欧盟之后，英国对欧盟的服务贸易顺差状态将难以延续；此外，金融业是英国最大的FDI流入行业，脱欧之后伦敦金融中心地位可能不保。当前欧盟<u>超过60%的欧元交易和全球超过40%的美元交易均在伦敦完成</u>，退出欧盟后，<u>英国境内大部分跨国金融机构可能主动从伦敦转移，大规模欧元交易也可能不再被允许，</u>届时伦敦的金融中心地位可能不保。

Source: Sina. (2016) 英国脱欧引发多米诺骨牌效应 *[Britain's Brexit triggers domino effect]*. Available at: http://finance.sina.com.cn/money/future/fmnews/2016-07-27/doc-ifxunyyf6033271.shtml?from=wap (Accessed: 11 April 2018)

Even if you cannot read Chinese, it is clear to see that there are large chunks of text that have been copied from the article. Although the characters are not a 100 per cent match, it is clear that minimal effort has been made to translate these sentences into the student's own words. This kind of machine/direct translation is not acceptable in academic writing and would be classed as misconduct. For your information, this particular student scored zero in this assessment.

NOTE: The same process can be used to locate machine/direct translations from any language, not only Chinese. The example above did not include references, but even if you do reference the source, if you did not translate the information yourself it is still recognised as academic malpractice.

Translations are paraphrases

Your translations should be done in the same way as a **paraphrase**. Read the source, understand its meaning, write down some notes (ideally in English), and then write down the ideas presented from your notes. Finally, do not forget to provide a citation and an entry in the reference list.

If you want to check against the original, follow the same procedure as in this unit. Translate your version back into your own language using software, then put this information into a search engine to check if the original source comes back in the results.

You can use software to translate individual words or short phrases, especially keywords, but that is the limit. Do not translate whole sentences or paragraphs, as it is your job to convey the original meaning into your own words.

Summary ✔

Courses that are taught in English will often encourage or even require you to conduct your research in English. There are some cases where foreign-language sources are unavoidable, and if you are able to locate a professionally translated source, then you should use this version as evidence in your essay. However, if a foreign-language source is required (and you cannot locate a pre-translated text), then make sure you translate the source yourself. Try to think of translations as paraphrases; by understanding the meaning of the source, you should be able to write out the ideas using your own words.

9.5 – Quotations

Keywords

Citation	Provided whenever evidence has been used in an essay. Part of the referencing process.
Cohesion	The flow of ideas connecting or uniting as a whole. Achieved through the use of keywords, linking phrases or grammar.
Paraphrase	The presentation of others' ideas in your own words.
Quotation marks	Punctuation used for reported speech. Provided at the beginning and end of any words copied from another source.
Reference list	Given at the end of an essay. Provides further details that are not given alongside the citation (eg book title, website URL).

Introduction

Although you are highly encouraged to use your own words in your papers, there are some occasions where direct copying is necessary. However, when doing this, the information should be presented in the form of a quotation. This method of giving evidence clearly signals to the reader that these words are not your own.

Using quotations

Quotations are most useful when you want to use the words that somebody said during an interview, or from a piece of well-written text containing expressions that would possibly lose their meaning during the **paraphrasing** process.

Therefore, quotations should only be used when every word that was said in the original text is important, and the overall meaning is far too complex to be paraphrased successfully.

As a general rule, quotations should be kept to a minimum and should only be used if relevant. If you can paraphrase or **summarise** the source, then use your own words. This will make the whole essay sound more **cohesive** and natural, as the writing will be continuously provided in your own style.

Rules of quotations

There are a few rules you should follow when using quotations in your papers.

» **Be exact** – copy the text as it appears in the original (including spelling).

» **Keep them short** – in-text quotations should be no longer than 20 words.

» **Use "quotation marks"** – when you copy somebody else's words, be sure to put them in "quotation marks". These can be 'single' or "double" quotation marks, just be consistent throughout.

» **Use referencing** – just like paraphrases and summaries, you must say where these ideas (and in these cases, words) came from. Provide **citations** and **reference list** entries.

» **Provide the page number** – if your quotation has come from a printed source or an e-document with multiple pages, you should also provide the page number as part of the citation.

NOTE: Paraphrases and summaries do not need quotation marks, but they must be provided with quotations. If you use a quotation without quotation marks, you will be accused of plagiarism, even if you have given references.

Breaking up quotations

Sometimes you may feel that copying an entire sentence is unnecessary, but there are small sections of a text that you do need to quote. In cases such as these, you write a sentence in your own words but also include short quotations throughout. For example:

> *Sam Gyimah, Universities Minister, described the change as 'a key milestone' and that 'not only will it benefit [...] graduates in the next financial year' but also 'millions in the years to come' (Department for Education, 2018).*

This example only presents the essential parts of the text and joins them together using minor transitional phrases. In the second quotation, the symbol [...] has been used to demonstrate that some text has been removed from the sentence. The original was: '*Not only will it benefit hundreds of thousands of graduates in the next financial year*'. The phrase '*hundreds of thousands*' was removed, as it was seen to be vague and unnecessary.

Longer quotations

In some longer papers, you may be required to supply extracts from documents (eg policies), reports, or key texts relating to the field of research. These extracts are classified as quotations, but they should be formatted in a different manner to a typical in-text quote.

» **Start on a new line of text** – just like starting a new paragraph.

» **Indent the quote** – leave some extra space on the left and right side of the page.

» **Cite at the end** – only provide a citation at the end of the quotation, not in-text.

» **Limit the length** – keep the quotation below five lines of text.

* Example

Avoiding the overuse of quotations in academic writing is something that many teachers have tried to communicate to their students. The book English for Academic Purposes: A Handbook for Students *suggests:*

> *As a general rule, quotations should be kept to a minimum and should only be used if relevant. If you can paraphrase or summarise the source, then use your own words. This will make the whole essay sound more cohesive and natural, as the writing will be continuously provided in your own style (Graham, 2018).*

Essentially, this means that students should aim to use their own words throughout their papers. By doing this, their writing will be far more cohesive for their readers to follow.

 NOTE: The formatting rules above only apply to longer quotations. Remember to avoid using long quotations in shorter papers (anything less than 3,000 words). Providing long quotations are tedious for the reader, and often unnecessary.

Word counts

Quotations do not count towards your essay's final word count. So, if you think you can use lots of quotations to reach the required limit set by your tutor, then you are wasting your time. Word counts only apply to your own words. Therefore, you have another reason to avoid using too many quotations and spend more time and effort on paraphrasing and summarising the ideas of others.

Summary ✓

Quotations are not considered the best way to provide evidence in an academic paper. However, they are not to be completely avoided, but simply kept to a minimum. You will be able to demonstrate a much deeper understanding of your topic if you use other methods of presenting evidence, such as paraphrasing and summarising. When you do need to use a quotation, just remember to keep them short, provide citations and place all of the copied words inside 'quotation marks'.

References

Department for Education (2018) *600,000 Graduates to Benefit from Financial Milestone*. Available at: www.gov.uk/government/news/600000-graduates-to-benefit-from-financial-milestone (Accessed: 11 April 2018).

9.6 – Reporting verbs

Keywords

Hedging — Cautious language that is used when presenting ideas that have some level of doubt regarding their validity or certainty.

Validity — The quality of being logical and reliable.

Introduction

When using the ideas (or even the words) of others in your papers, reporting verbs are a key element for introducing and outlining that the information has come from evidence. For many students, the difficulty with using reporting verbs is that there are many to choose from and each of them has a slightly different meaning.

Choosing the right verb

When using evidence in your papers, you are presenting ideas that you want to highlight to your reader, evaluate their meaning, or possibly show that you agree or disagree with the author's view. Reporting verbs are useful as they can express how you view the evidence and how you are going to use the information in your argument.

The chosen verb not only indicates how you plan to use the evidence, but it also expresses your view on the **validity** of the claims they make. Furthermore, if you are using evidence that includes an author's perspective on somebody else's idea, the reporting verb can also be used to express their point of view.

Hedging plays a vital role in the way you provide evidence, as you need to evaluate the source and decide how strong the author's claims are (by how well supported their articles are). If you feel there is any doubt about an idea or claim you are presenting, be sure to use reporting verbs that show caution.

Here is a table of reporting verbs that have been split into categories of purpose and strength of claim:

Purpose	Cautious	Neutral	Strong
Addition		adds	
Advice		advises	
Agreement	admits, concedes	accepts, acknowledges, agrees, confirms, recognises	applauds, congratulates, praises, supports

Purpose	Cautious	Neutral	Strong
Argument	apologises	assures, encourages, interprets, justifies, reasons	argues, contents, convinces, emphasises, insists, proves, warns
Believing	guesses, hopes, imagines	believes, claims, declares, expresses, feels, holds, maintains	asserts, guarantees, upholds
Conclusion		concludes, discovers, finds, infers, realises	
Disagreement or questioning	doubts	challenges, debates, disagrees, questions, requests	accuses, attacks, contradicts, criticises, denies, discounts, dismisses, disputes, opposes, refutes, rejects
Discussion	comments	discusses, explores	reasons
Emphasis			highlights, stresses
Evaluate or examine		analyses, assesses, compares, considers, evaluates, examines, investigates, understands	blames, complains, ignores, scrutinises
Explanation		clarifies, explains	
Presentation	confuses	comments, defines, describes, estimates, identifies, illustrates, implies, informs, mentions, notes, observes, outlines, points out, presents, restates, reveals, shows, states	announces, promises
Suggestion	alleges, speculates	advises, hypothesises, proposes, suggests, theorises	asserts, recommends, urges

Adapted from University of Adelaide (2014).

English for Academic Purposes: A Handbook for Students

Tenses

Reporting verbs are more commonly provided in the *present simple* form, especially in argumentative essays that make use of the most recent resources. However, you may also use the *past tense* when providing research that has been completed, including recent findings in research studies that are no longer ongoing.

* Example – present tense

Graham (2018) stresses that reporting verbs are essential when providing evidence, especially quotations.

* Example – past tense

Scientists observed significant changes in the subjects' behaviour (Smith, 2015).

Grammatical structure

There are two commonly used structures that reporting verbs appear in, with the majority of the verbs working in both forms. However, note that some verbs will only work in one of the two structures.

* Structure 1: Verb + noun (noun phrase)

Jones (2006) expresses strong disapproval of the current administration's policies.

* Structure 2: Verb + that + clause

Baker (2012) identified that the increased number of failures was due to a lack of clarity in the assignment brief.

Summary ✔

Reporting verbs are not only useful for indicating that you are referring to the ideas of others, but also for conveying your (or the author's) view on the claim being made. Remember, reporting verbs can be presented in several different forms, but some will not work in every sentence.

The details provided in this unit should be enough to get you started with using reporting verbs in your essays. However, to learn more about their use, take a look at the further reading suggestions provided below, and pay attention to how others use reporting verbs in the articles you read during your research.

References

University of Adelaide (2014) *Verbs for Reporting*. Available at: www.adelaide.edu.au/writingcentre/docs/learningGuide_verbsForReporting.pdf (Accessed: 12 April 2018).

Further reading

For more details about reporting verbs, check out the following resources:

Education First (no date) *Reporting Verbs*. Available at: www.ef.com/english-resources/english-grammar/reporting-verbs (Accessed: 13 July 2018).

Swan, M. (2016) *Practical English Usage*. 4th edn. Oxford: Oxford University Press.

Unit 10
Referencing

10.1 – Understanding referencing

Keywords

Academic misconduct	A term used to describe cheating in education, such as stealing other people's words or ideas.
Assignment brief	A document outlining details such as the assessment task, deadlines, and how the work will be graded.
Bibliography	A list of sources that contributed to the formation of ideas in an essay, but were not directly used as evidence in the paper.
Citation	Provided whenever evidence has been used in an essay. Part of the referencing process.
Harvard referencing	The most commonly used style of referencing used globally and across a large majority of subjects.
Reference list	Given at the end of an essay. Provides further details that are not given alongside the citation (eg book title, website URL).

Introduction

While studying in higher education, you will be required to produce work that is not only based on your own ideas but is backed up by research. You will be encouraged to undertake further reading into your subject and gather a range of sources that will aid in the formation of your ideas. However, you cannot take all the credit for these newly created ideas, as you will need to provide details regarding where you collected the information that aided in the formation of these new ideas.

Avoiding plagiarism

There are many reasons for including references in your papers, but the biggest reason is to avoid the accusation of plagiarism. If you are seen to be using the words, or even ideas, of others without informing the reader where this information has come from, then you are committing **academic misconduct**. Essentially, you are trying to convince the reader that you are the creator of this idea or string of words, when the truth is you have 'stolen' this information from somebody else.

This form of academic misconduct can take many forms, but here are some examples of what most universities would classify as plagiarism.

» Presenting the words of others in your work without reference. This can come from any source, including your peers.

» Using the exact words of others (quotation), with a reference, but without placing the copied words inside 'quotation marks'.

» Paraphrasing or summarising an idea without providing references to the original source.

» Reusing your own work from a previous assessment (also known as 'self-plagiarism').

» Providing references to sources that either do not exist, or do not provide the idea or words you present in your work (also known as 'falsifying sources').

Other reasons to reference

Avoiding plagiarism is not the only reason for providing references in your papers. Some other valid reasons for including references are given here.

» **Demonstrate understanding** – by including references, you are informing the reader that you have taken the time to understand the topic by reading into the wider subject.

» **Provide direction** – your references are signposts that direct the reader to where your information has been collected. This allows them to check your sources and do some further reading.

» **Show appreciation** – acknowledging where your ideas have come from shows that you respect the work of others and want to give credit for their contributions to the topic.

» **Highlight your contributions** – references inform the reader which parts of the essay are your own and those that are taken from elsewhere. Therefore, this provides a clear indication of what contributions you have made to the topic.

Reference everything?

The list of what should be referenced in your essays is extremely long, and some examples of what this includes will be provided throughout this set of units. However, there are some things that do not need a reference.

Personal experience

In an academic paper, it is rare that you will be able to provide personal examples of your experiences. However, sometimes you will be required to write a reflective essay, and in these cases, you will not need to reference your own experiences. However, you will be expected to relate your experience to an idea or theory.

Common knowledge

Ideas that are commonly known do not need to be referenced in your paper. However, this is sometimes difficult to judge, as the concept of 'common knowledge' will vary based on factors such as location (ie educational background and culture) and the subject you are studying. Therefore, you will need to consider who your audience is going to be before deciding if references are required.

Some examples of common knowledge are the name of a country's capital city, the number of days in a week, basic mathematics (eg 2 + 2 = 4), and the order of the planets in our solar system.

If you have only just learnt something, or you feel the need to look at a source to check if the idea is correct, then it probably means you will need to provide a reference. Sometimes, it may be safer to check with your tutor before submitting a final version of your essay that includes what you believe to be 'common knowledge'.

Styles of referencing

While conducting research, you may come across several different referencing styles, such as APA, Chicago, and MLA. However, the style that is most prevalent is known as Harvard referencing. In this book, the Harvard referencing style will be presented throughout, but it is worth noting that many of these styles of formatting do share some similarities in the information required and the way they are presented as **citations** and **reference lists**. Therefore, if your tutor requires you to use a different style, your knowledge of Harvard referencing should make the process of learning this new style much easier.

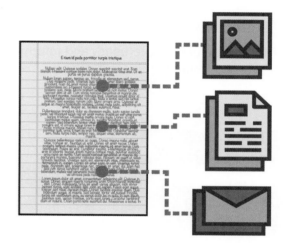

Reference lists versus bibliographies

Often these two names are used interchangeably for the list of source details provided at the end of a paper. However, there is a slight difference between these two methods of referencing. The reference list provides details of all sources used and cited in the paper, whereas a bibliography also includes sources that were read and contributed in some way to the formation of ideas or arguments, but were not directly used as evidence anywhere in the paper. In other words, you will need to provide a list of all sources that you found to be useful, even if they have not been cited in your essay.

Usually, the **assignment brief** states if you should present a reference list, a bibliography, or both (as separate sections). However, if you are unable to locate clear instructions regarding what is expected, then be sure to check with your tutor.

Note-taking: what information do I need?

Writing your citations and reference lists can be an easy task if you have all the relevant details available in one location. The best place for this is in the notes you have made while conducting research. A common mistake made by students is to gather research, but not the source details. This results in students wasting time trying to find the information again, just for a few details.

The information you are required to make notes on does vary between the different types of sources, but here is a list of some of the most common details you will be required to collect.

Author's name	Name of organisation
Title	Publisher details
Date of publication	Website address *(URL)*
Edition, volume, issue	Date accessed *(when you found it)*

How these details are used, and information about what other possible notes you may need to make, will be covered throughout this set of units.

Summary ✔

Referencing is not a difficult skill to master as there are many guides written about how references are given and formatted. It may start out as a time-consuming process, but as you become more familiar with referencing, you will be able to write out your citations and reference lists with relative ease. When it comes to deciding what to reference, a general rule to follow is 'reference everything'. Providing some ideas that you consider to be common knowledge without references may be risky, and you would be upset to find your work scores zero just because you missed out a few references.

Furthermore, it is also worth noting that referencing is not only used in academic papers. You will be required to provide references in other assessments completed in higher education, such as presentations.

Keywords

Reference list	Given at the end of an essay. Provides further details that are not given alongside the citation (eg book title, website URL).
Reporting verb	Verbs used to introduce the words or ideas of others (ie reported speech). Used when providing evidence in an essay.

Introduction

Referencing comes in two parts, with a few details of your sources being provided in the main text of your essay, and further information being presented at the very end of the paper. The citation is the name given to the details you provide in your essay's paragraphs. This is primarily used to inform the reader of when and where evidence has been used.

Elements of a citation

Citations usually include the following pieces of information.

» **Author's family name** – also known as their 'surname'.

» **Year of publication** – this should be the year the source was printed (eg books/journals/magazines) or made available online (eg web article/e-book/e-journal/video).

Citation styles

There are two different styles of citations you can provide in your work. In both cases, the reader is informed that evidence is being offered, but their attention is directed towards either the source or idea.

Focus on the idea (end-of-text citation)

When you aim to focus on the idea or claim rather than the source of the information, you can provide an 'end-of-text' citation. For this style, you will need to place all the citation's details (author and year) in brackets at the end of the sentence.

*When evidence is used in academic papers, students are reminded to inform the reader of where the information was initially located (**Graham, 2016**).*

Focus on the source (in-text citation)

For this style of citation, you are emphasising the source of the idea. This does not mean the idea is not important, but the authority of the author or organisation helps provide further validity to your own claims.

In this case, the author's name will be provided as part of the sentence, followed by the year in brackets. Furthermore, this style of citation also utilises **reporting verbs** before the author's idea or claim is presented.

Smith (2014) recommended the use of reliable sources in academic papers...

Formatting citations

The rest of this unit will cover various citation formats you may need to use in your own papers. For each format, you will notice examples provided as both *'in-text'* and *'end-of-text'* citations.

Citing two or three authors (same source)

When there are two authors for a single source, both family names are provided.

Parker and Lewis (2008) proposed the idea that all professionals should...

....their contribution is recognised internationally (Parker, Lewis and Chen, 2008).

Citing four or more authors (same source)

To avoid writing long lists of names, when there are four or more authors, you should provide the family name of the first author listed followed by *'et al.'* (which means *'and others'*).

Wells et al. (2007) believe that universities should provide their students with...

...this will inevitably lead to a reduction in the number of failures (Wells et al., 2007).

Citing multiple sources

The names of each source will follow the same format as above. List the sources in chronological order (oldest to newest), with sources published in the same year provided alphabetically by author. Note that *'end-of-text'* citations should be separated by a semicolon.

Daniels (2010), Williams et al. (2010) and Garner (2013) identified that...

...eventually losing money (Daniels, 2010; Williams et al., 2010; Garner, 2013).

Citing sources with the same author and year of publication

There will be occasions when you use evidence provided by an author who has published multiple articles in a single year. Alternatively, you may also be referencing an organisation that has published several useful texts in the same year. For these cases, add a lowercase letter after the year starting with 'a' and continuing alphabetically.

Reeves (2001a) argues that this change... Additionally, Reeves (2001b) adds that...

...down by 20 per cent (Reeves, 2001a). ...nearly half of all adults (Reeves, 2001b).

Remember to also provide the lowercase letter in the **reference list** entry alongside the year of publication. This is necessary to let the reader know where and when you have used each source.

Citing secondary sources

While reading your sources, you will sometimes notice references to evidence the author has used. If there are any ideas presented as evidence in the source you are reading that you wish to use in your paper, you will need to reference both authors' names in your citation.

Evens (2013, cited in Cook, 2016) highlights the importance of research into...

...these skills will allow for a stronger workforce (Evens, 2013, cited in Cook, 2016).

There are a few other points to consider about using secondary sources.

» If the information you want to use was presented as a quotation (not a paraphrase or summary), then instead of *'cited in'* use the phrase *'quoted in'*: *(Evens, 2013, quoted in Cook, 2016).*

» In your reference list, you will only need to provide an entry for the source you have read. This means you do not need to write an entry for the original source of the idea, but you still need to give their details in the citation.

» If you can access the source that is cited, you should go and read that text instead, as this will allow you to provide a direct reference. However, do not provide a direct citation to the original if you have not actually read the source.

Citing sources with page numbers

In some cases, you will also need to provide page numbers in your citation. Direct quotations taken from books or journals are the most comment example of this requirement.

Doyle (2017, p. 113) discusses the potential issues that occur when dealing with...

...with drastic changes taking place in their personalities (Doyle, 2017, p. 113).

Citing sources with no author

Sources that are provided online sometimes are not assigned an individual author. In many cases there will be an organisation (or at the least, a company) responsible for publishing the source, and this can serve as a replacement for the author.

> *Statistics provided by ONS (2017) suggest that the unemployment is on the rise...*
>
> *...the United States, but they are holding steady in most Asian nations (ONS, 2017).*

However, in some very rare cases, an article may not state an author or organisation. If you are planning to use these sources in your essay, then replace the author with the title.

> *The article 'Teamwork in the Workplace' (2003) provides several suggestions...*
>
> *...communications may break down (Teamwork in the Workplace, 2003).*

 NOTE: Do not use phrases like 'Unknown' or 'Anonymous' if the author or organisation cannot be identified. As mentioned above, the title of the article will serve as a better replacement in your citations.

Citing sources with no year of publication

If a source does not offer you a date of publication in any form, then you will need to replace the year of publication with the phrase *'no date'*.

> *Morrison (no date) promises to provide the community with an increased number...*
> *...reduce the pressure placed on current transportation links (Morrison, no date).*

Citing sources with non-English-named authors

When dealing with non-English names, you need to make sure that when you provide these in your references you use a Romanised version of their name. For example, a Chinese name would need to be presented in Pinyin (eg Zhang Min).

As mentioned previously, the name provided in the citation should be the author's family name. This can sometimes be difficult to identify because in some countries given names are provided first and the family name comes second, but in others this is reversed. Providing the family name first is most common in Asian counties, such as China, Japan, Vietnam and Korea.

Here are some other nationalities where identifying family names may be challenging.

» **Portuguese** – the given name comes first but is then followed by two family names. First is the mother's family name, then the father's. You should only reference the father's family name in your citation.

» **Spanish and Latin America** – similar to Portuguese, the given name comes first and is followed by two family names. However, this time the father's family name comes first, then the mother's. For these names, reference both parents' family names.

In Unit 10.3 you will find some examples of how to format non-English names in your references. However, if you are ever in doubt, then speak to your tutor for advice about naming conventions. In some cases, a quick search online should be able to provide you with an answer (eg search using the term *'formatting Chinese names referencing'*).

Summary ✔

Although citations do not include many details, their purpose is significant. They are essential for avoiding plagiarism but are not a guarantee. Furthermore, citations help differentiate which sections are your ideas and which are those of others. As a final piece of advice, include your citations in your essay while writing. Do not wait until you have finished the paper, then go back and add your citations because you may forget to include one or two, and this will result in accusations of plagiarism.

Further reading

For more details about citations (and reference lists), check out the following resources:

Pears, R. and Shields, G. (2016) *Cite Them Right*. 10th edn. London: Palgrave.

Williams, K. and David, M. (2017) *Referencing and Understanding Plagiarism*. 2nd edn. London: Palgrave.

10.3 – Reference lists

Keywords

Citation   Provided whenever evidence has been used in an essay. Part of the referencing process.

e-Book   An electronic version of a book.

Edition   A version of a printed text, usually used for books.

Publisher   A company responsible for printing and distributing books.

Transcript   A written record of spoken text (eg interview).

Introduction

The purpose of the reference list is to allow the reader to easily find the sources that you used in your work. The details provided in a reference list can vary depending on the type of source that has been used, and this unit will cover the most commonly used types of sources you are likely to encounter.

Author's name

In a reference list, the author's name is provided in a slightly different form to the **citation**. In the reference list, you will also need to supply the first letter of any given names (also known as their *'initials'*). See the following table for some examples of how names should be presented.

Author's name	In-text citation	End-of-text citation	Reference list entry
Pauline Hayes	Hayes (2005) states…	(Hayes, 2005).	Hayes, P. (2005) *Title.*
Pittman, Sarah Jane	Pittman (2014) states…	(Pittman, 2014).	Pittman, S. J. (2014) *Title.*
Chinese names			
Xiang Zemin	Xiang (2011) states…	(Xiang, 2011).	Xiang, Z. (2011) *Title.*

Author's name	In-text citation	End-of-text citation	Reference list entry
Vietnamese names			
Võ Nguyên Giáp	Võ (1975) states...	(Võ, 1975)	Võ, N. G. (1975) *Title.*
Portuguese names			
Armando Gonçalves Pereira	Pereira (1949) states...	(Pereira, 1949).	Pereira, A. G. (1949) *Title.*
Spanish/Latin American names			
Pedro Vallina Martínez	Vallina Martínez (1986) states...	(Vallina Martínez, 1986).	Vallina Martínez, P. (1986) *Title.*

NOTE: For sources that have more than one author, follow the same format as covered in Unit 9.2, with the inclusion of their initials. For example: 'Parker, F., Lewis, A. D., and Chen, M.' or 'Wells, S. et al.'.

Non-English titles

Most reference list entries will require you to provide a title (eg book title, article title, and journal title). If you are going to use a source that is written in another language, you will need to provide a translation [in square brackets] alongside the original title.

> Liu, M. (2005) *Xin jianqiao sangwu yingyu (Zhongji)* [New Cambridge Business English (Intermediate)]. Beijing: Posts and Telecom Press.

Referencing books

Although you can gain many details from the front cover of a book, the best place to look is in the first few pages. Here you should be able to locate the following.

» Author's name(s).

» Year of publication.

» Title of book.

» Edition *(only needed if it is not the first edition)*.

» Publisher's name and address.

Take a look at the following example and notice when details have been presented in *italics*, the location of punctuation (brackets, full stops and colons) and the use of 'edn' to represent 'edition'.

---

* Format

Surname, Initials. (Year) *Title of book.* Edition. Place of Publication: Publisher.

* Examples

Pears, R. and Shields, G. (2016) *Cite them right.* 10th edn. London: Palgrave.

Redman, P. (2006) *Good essay writing: A social science guide.* 3rd edn. London: Open University.

For e-books, the details are almost the same. In fact, if the version of your e-book looks exactly like a printed version (possibly in PDF format), then you can reference it in the same way. However, if your e-book version was downloaded to an e-reader, such as a Kindle or iPad, then you will need to provide the following details.

» URL *(downloaded location)*;

» Date you downloaded the e-book.

---

* Format

Family Name, Initials. (Year) *Title of book.* Available at: URL (Downloaded: Date Month Year).

* Example

Machin, L. et al. (2016) *A complete guide to the level 5 diploma in education and training.* 2nd edn. Available at: http://a.co/75NTK27 (Downloaded: 15 March 2017).

Referencing journal articles

Journal articles provide some of the same information as books, but require further details to help locate them.

» Author's name(s).

» Year of publication.

» Title of article.

» Title of journal.

» Volume, issue and/or month.

» Page numbers.

Again, look at the examples and pay attention to the use of punctuation and formatting.

> *** Format**
>
> Family Name, Initials. (Year) 'Title of article', *Title of Journal,* Volume (Issue/Month), pp. Start Page – Finishing Page.
>
> *** Example**
>
> Boughton, J. M. (2002) 'The Bretton Woods proposal: an in-depth look', *Political Science Quarterly,* 42(6), pp. 564–578.

If you located your journal article online, then you will need to provide one of the following pieces of information.

» URL and accessed date.

» Digital Object Identifier *(doi).*

These details then need to be included into the reference using the following format.

> *** Format**
>
> Family Name, Initials. (Year) 'Title of article', *Title of Journal,* Volume (Issue/Month), pp. Start Page – Finishing Page. Available at: URL (Accessed: Date Month Year).
>
> Family Name, Initials. (Year) 'Title of article', *Title of Journal,* Volume (Issue/Month), pp. Start Page – Finishing Page. doi: ##.####/###########.
>
> *** Examples**
>
> Orr, K. and Simmons, R. (2010) 'Dual identities: the in-service teacher trainee experience in English further education sector', *Journal of Vocational Education and Training,* 62(1), pp. 75–88. Available at: www.tandfonline.com/doi/full/10.1080/13636820903452650 (Accessed: 16 April 2014).
>
> Whitty, G. (2008) 'Twenty years of progress? English education policy 1998 to the present', *Education Management Administration Leadership,* 36(2), pp. 165–184. doi: 10.1177/1741143207087771.

Referencing websites

Looking for the required referencing details on many websites can be a challenging task, and some advice on how to do this is covered in Unit 7.4. In most cases, when referring to websites, you will need to identify the following pieces of information.

» Author's name(s) *(or organisation).*

» Year of publication *(when the information was posted online).*

» Title of article/web page.

» URL and date accessed.

Referencing online videos

Online videos now provide access to material such as documentaries and lectures. For these sources, the format is basically the same as referencing a website, but the details of the author are slightly different.

» Name(s) of creator/presenter *(the person or organisation who hosts the video)*.

» Year of post *(when it was made available online)*.

» Title of video.

» URL and date accessed.

Referencing lectures (and material)

Sometimes you will have gained ideas or material through a lecture. This may be covered during examples or via slideshow presentations (eg PowerPoint Slides). Here are the details required to reference a lecture.

» Lecturer/tutor's name(s).

» Year of lecture.

» Title *(the focus of the lecture)*.

» Medium *(how the lecture was given)*.

» Module code *(if known)* and name.

» Location *(name of college or university)*.

» Date and month.

---

* Format

Family Name, Initials. (Year) *Title/Focus of lecture* [Medium], *Module Code: Module Name.* Name of College or University. Date and Month.

* Example

Limburg, D. (2018) *Ethical practices* [Lecture to Level 5 BSc Accounting], *U50040: Research in Accounting.* Oxford Brookes University. 22 February.

If you want to refer to any material made available for you to download via your student website (eg Blackboard or Moodle) then you will need to include the following details.

» File type *(instead of medium)*.

» URL and date accessed *(instead of location and date/month)*.

---

* Format

Family Name, Initials. (Year) *Title/Focus of Lecture* [File Type]. *Module Code: Module Name.* Available at: URL (Accessed: Date Month Year).

* Example

Crosbie, P. (2015) *Sampling* [PowerPoint Presentation]. *BUS2801: Research Methods.* Available at: https://student.zy.cdut.edu.cn/resource/2015-11/ppt-sampling (Accessed: 20 November 2015).

Referencing interviews

If you wish to reference interviews in your work, you will require the following details.

» Name(s) of person interviewed.

» Year of interview.

» Title of interview *(if any)*.

» Name of interviewer.

» Name of publication or broadcaster.

» Date and month of interview, and page number *(if relevant)*.

For interviews found online, include the *'URL'* and *'Date Accessed'* at the end of the reference.

For interviews conducted by yourself, omit details such as *'Name of Publisher or Broadcaster'* and any details referring to the location (eg *Page Numbers* or *URL*). Provide your full name after the phrase *'Interviewed by'*.

NOTE: For primary research you will need to provide access to the information for your readers. For example, you can present a **transcript** of your interview at the end of your paper, or a URL link to a voice/video recording.

Alphabetical order

Reference lists need to be organised alphabetically by the author's name. Sources that have the same author can be listed in chronological order (oldest to newest). For sources that have the same author and same year, provide the entries in the same order they appear in your work, and also provide a lowercase letter after the publication year (starting with *'a'* and continuing alphabetically).

* Example

Brookfield, S. (1995) *Becoming a Critically Reflective Teacher.* San Francisco, CA: Jossey-Bass.

Gibbs, G. (1988) *Learning by Doing: A Guide to Teaching and Learning Methods.* Oxford: Further Educational Unit – Oxford Polytechnic.

LSIS *(2013a) Teaching and Training Qualification for the Further Education and Skills Sector in England.* Coventry: Learning Skills Improvement Services.

LSIS *(2013b) Qualifications Guidance for Awarding Organisations.* Coventry: Learning Skills Improvement Services.

Rust, C. *(2000) Principles of Assessment.* York: HEA.

Rust, C. *(2002) Purposes and Principles of Assessment.* Oxford: Oxford Brookes University.

Summary ✓

This unit has introduced a range of commonly referenced sources in academic work, but the list of sources you could reference is far more extensive. However, if you cannot locate the formatting rules for a source you have found, websites like *Cite This for Me* and *Cite Them Right Online* can offer guidance for a wide range of sources.

When looking for instructions on formatting your reference lists, you may notice some minor differences between how some books or websites format their entries. There is no problem following these suggested formats as long as it still shares similarities with the Harvard referencing system. The critical thing to remember is to be consistent with your own reference lists. For example, how you format one entry for a book should be the same format you use for all books in your reference list.

Unit 11
Revision techniques

11.1 – Feedback

Keywords

Assessment task	Details of what you are expected to do in your assignment. Could be provided in the form of a question.
Deadline	The date and time when your final version must be submitted for grading.
Draft	An early version of an essay. Usually, multiple drafts are created before the final draft (which is submitted for grading).
Learning outcome	A statement that describes the knowledge or skill that should be gained through a module or assessment.
Marking criteria	Details how an assignment is divided up (usually represented as a percentage).
Marking rubric	Primarily used by teachers to grade assessments. These provide the targets for each criteria and define the difference between pass and fail (and other grade boundaries).
Self-assessment	A process of reviewing and reflecting on your work.
Submission	The act of delivering your work to your tutor for grading.

Introduction

Upon completing **drafts** of your papers, you should seek feedback from somewhere. This can be from your tutors, your peers, or via self-assessment. When receiving feedback from others, it is important that you understand what guidance is being offered, and that you formulate ways to address any issues raised.

Level of feedback versus expectations

Your tutor will often have to read papers submitted by many students, and this can be very time-consuming. Therefore, your tutor will likely provide very brief comments to guide you, and these will often only address areas that have the greatest influence on your score (either sections that are done exceptionally well, or areas that need more attention).

Many students often expect feedback on all aspects of their paper, such as areas where grammar mistakes have been made and how to fix them. This is an unrealistic expectation, as tutors would need to spend far longer on each paper than they have time for. You need to remember that your tutors have deadlines too and they need to return the work to all students by a certain date.

English for Academic Purposes: A Handbook for Students

When studying in higher education, you are required to be more independent, which means you have to be able to accept the guidance you are given, but also put in the extra effort to find solutions to any issues you might have in your work. However, if there is any feedback given that you do not understand, then you must ask your tutor for more details. Ask questions in tutorials, send emails or go to see them during their office hours.

Assignment briefs

Most of the time, your tutors will point you towards the assignment brief when they feel your work is missing something or is possibly not on track to achieve a passing grade. For details on what can be found in an assignment brief, and how to better understand your assessment task, please refer to Unit 2.1. However, here is a brief description of the key areas you should be aware of.

Deadline and submission details

Usually provided at the very start of an assignment brief. Use the deadline to manage your time effectively and be sure to allow time for your work to be checked before submission. Pay attention to what your tutors are expecting you to submit (eg file types) and how it is to be provided (as a printed or electronic copy).

Learning outcomes

These are provided as a list of aims that relate to the overall learning experience. These skills should be achieved by completing the assessment. For example, if the learning outcome is *'Engage in self-directed activity with guidance/evaluation'*, this means that each student should be able to create a piece of work independently with only minimal input from their tutors.

Assessment task

This is where the requirements are outlined. Often presented in quite an academic form, it is important to read this section carefully and break down the task into its components (*task* and *focus words*). Ask your tutor any specific questions you may have about the task, but do not ask them *'what do I need to do?'*, as they will often not answer this question directly.

Marking criteria

The marking criteria outlines how the assessment is weighted. This is usually done by giving a percentage to each area of assessment, making it very clear to the student which areas require careful consideration. For example, if your assessment has a high percentage assigned to the *Structure* criteria, you will need to pay attention to the presentation of information in your essay (ie use of cohesive devices, such as thesis statement and topic sentences).

Marking rubric

Possibly the most important part of the assignment brief, and a great source of reference for interpreting feedback. Your tutors use this information to grade your work, so you should be able to see why a tutor has highlighted a particular area as needing attention. Rubrics can sometimes appear quite confusing but do take some time to read them carefully and you will begin to find ways to improve your work.

Feedback terminology

The following table contains some comments your tutors may leave on your work. Each comment has been explained in detail to help you understand what your tutors are highlighting.

Comment	Meaning
'Insufficient evidence' or 'Weak support'	You have presented an idea or claim with evidence that does not offer enough support. The reason may be the source is of poor quality or it is not clearly related to the point you are trying make.
'Does not answer question'	Your ideas do not help answer the question provided in the assignment brief. Take a closer look at the assessment task and make sure you have broken it down into task and focus words. Be sure to stay on topic and do not provide too much description (as this can often lead to you straying off topic).
'Does not support argument'	The ideas and evidence you provide should support the thesis. For example, if you are going to argue that China is a better investment for businesses than the US, then make sure you give reasons why this is true. If you do mention any reasons why the US is a better investment, then make sure you counter-argue these points with a rebuttal.
'Confusing structure'	This usually means that you have not provided information in the correct order. For example, maybe you have given a piece of evidence before introducing the supporting point. Or maybe your main body paragraphs are not provided in a cohesive order.
'Grammar errors'	Tutors in higher education will not give you advice on correcting your grammar during their feedback (this is your job, as part of the proofreading process). However, they will point out areas where your grammar is causing difficulties in understanding.
'Good attempt at...' or 'Clear attempt at...'	Sometimes your tutor will comment that you have made a good attempt at something (maybe structure, or providing evidence), but this does not mean it is perfect. This means you are heading in the right direction and you should continue to push yourself to improve these areas.
'Missing references'	This usually means that citations are missing, or an entry is missing in the reference list. You should provide details of all your evidence, where it has been used (via citations) and where to locate the source (via the reference list).

Peer- and self-assessment

In higher education, you should not only rely on your tutors for feedback. With a little bit of guidance, you and your peers can identify areas for improvement in your work. This process will help develop your understanding and to become more active in the overall learning process.

Peer and self-assessment are not about assigning a grade to a piece of work but are more focused on identifying the requirements and then checking to see if these have been met. The assignment brief provides all the relevant details to help you form a checklist that can guide you and your peers while assessing.

It is important to know the limits of peer and self-assessment, and that this will likely change as you progress through your course. When starting out, checking for how well you have explored a topic will be difficult to assess, as your peers' and your own understanding may be limited. However, it will be very easy for you and your peers to check if evidence has been presented alongside any claims made, and if referencing has also been formatted correctly. In later years, you will then be able to comment on other areas as your knowledge of the subject develops.

Peer assessment allows for you to hear feedback from a different point of view, and it may even present you with new ideas for exploration. Furthermore, if you get the opportunity to look at a peer's paper, you will see examples of areas where they have done well or have made errors. This will also aid in developing your work, as you will learn from both their strengths and mistakes.

 NOTE: Be careful when sharing work with peers. If you, or your peers, are tempted to copy any material relating to claims or research, then you may be accused of cheating. If possible, try to work together with a peer who may not be writing exactly the same topic as you, thus lowering the risk of ideas being stolen.

Forming a checklist

The marking rubric has all the necessary details for you and your peers to assess a piece of work. Below is part of a marking rubric for an academic paper.

Criteria: topic (30%)

Distinction (70–100%)	Merit (60–69%)	Pass (40–59%)	Fail (0–39%)
Has provided an answer to all three questions.	Has answered two out of three questions.	Has only answered one of the questions in sufficient detail.	Has not sufficiently answered any of the questions provided.
Every answer is supported by at least two sources.	Every answer is supported by at least one source.	Has provided support, but from a questionable source.	Has not used any reliable sources to support answers.

Distinction (70–100%)	Merit (60–69%)	Pass (40–59%)	Fail (0–39%)
Has provided counter-arguments for every claim.	Has provided at least one counter-argument.	Highlights a possible counter-argument but does not explore in detail.	Does not mention any counter-arguments.

In the criteria for topic, you can see there are three areas that will be graded by your tutor.

» Answers provided to questions.

» Evidence is used to support answers.

» The use of counter-arguments.

This information can then help structure a checklist for both peer and self-assessment. All you need to do is turn the information above into questions.

---

* Example

Is there an answer provided for all three questions?
Is every answer supported by two pieces of evidence from different sources?
Is there a counter-argument and rebuttal for every claim made?

Once you have written your paper, you or your peer can then use this checklist to see if you have met the requirements of the marking rubric. If the answer to all three questions is yes, then you should be on track for a strong score in the 'topic' criteria. However, if the answer is no, then it is up to you or your peer to highlight where this has not been done in the essay. From here you can make revisions until you can answer all three questions with a yes.

Summary ✔

Gathering feedback is essential for you to make suitable revisions to your work. Make sure you allow plenty of time for work to be checked and revised long before the submission deadline. In higher education, your tutors will provide you with some guidance, but you are expected to be more independent. This means you cannot expect detailed feedback that highlights every necessary improvement.

Pay attention to the details in the assignment briefs, as these will not only aid in your understanding of your tutor's comments but also allow for peer and self-assessment. Through creating a checklist, you and your peers should be able to identify areas for improvement. Furthermore, peer feedback allows you to get an insight into how your peers have approached the assignment and can expose areas in your own work that can be improved upon.

11.2 – Improving cohesion

Keywords

Concluding sentence	Used to signal that the current idea has been explored in sufficient detail.
Discourse marker	Words or phrases used to connect different sentences or clauses.
Thesis statement	A sentence provided in the introduction paragraph. This will outline the main claim of the entire essay.
Topic sentence	A sentence given at the start of each main body paragraph to express the main idea that will be explored within.

Introduction

Once you have gathered feedback on your work, you can then begin to make revisions. When writing the first draft of an essay, often the focus is on getting all your ideas onto paper, which means the structure and cohesion is usually a little untidy. This leads to errors in the way your claims are presented, or a more serious issue relating to the clarity of meaning. These problems can usually be fixed by addressing sentence length and variety issues, and/or the inclusion of **discourse markers**.

Sentence variety

If you are in the habit of writing sentences in patterns that all look alike, your papers may become monotonous to the reader despite your interesting ideas. To keep your readers interested and to express your varied thoughts, you need to use a variety of sentence patterns.

Take a look at the following paragraph and see if you can identify what the problem is.

> *Apple is a company. It is from America. It makes technological goods. It has been around for about 40 years. It makes popular devices such as the iPhone. They also make computers and tablets. At one point, their most famous product was the iPod. It was a small music player. It was very portable. They used to produce many different versions. Now they only have the iPod Touch. Their products are often seen to be too expensive. They continue to be a stable company worldwide.*

This paragraph uses a very repetitive pattern, starting most sentences with either *'it'* or *'they/their'*. Furthermore, each sentence uses a basic grammatical structure, with no sentence containing more than ten words. As mentioned previously, this kind of writing is not only dull for the reader but can also begin to cause confusion.

If you only provide ideas in short bursts of text, your reader will struggle to see the connection from one sentence to the next. By the end of the paragraph, your reader may have even forgotten what the aim of the entire paragraph is.

Combining sentences

One approach to reducing these short and monotonous sentences is through combining sentences to form a more complete, informative and interesting statement. Try to apply the following rules.

» Remove any repetitive words that appear in both sentences.

» Place descriptive words in front of the words they are describing.

» Connect similar sentences with words such as *'and'*, *'or'* and *'but'*.

---

* Example

» *Apple is a company. It is from America. It makes technological goods.*

   Apple is an American company that makes technological goods.

» *Their most famous product was the iPod. It was a small music player. It was very portable.*

   Their most famous product was a small, portable music player called the iPod.

» *Their products are often seen to be very expensive. They continue to be a stable company worldwide.*

   Their products are often seen to be too expensive, but they continue to be a stable company worldwide.

Coordinating conjunctions

Conjunctions are words used to join sentences/clauses together. Previously, the coordinating conjunctions *'and'*, *'or'* and *'but'* were mentioned, but you could also use *'so'*, *'yet'*, *'nor'* and *'for'*. However, you need to be careful in your choice as each conjunction has its own meaning.

Conjunction	Meaning	Conjunction	Meaning
and	Adds more information.	**or**	Presents a choice/ alternative.
but	Offers contrasting idea or introduces something unexpected.	**so**	Similar to the phrase *'therefore'* or *'as a result'*.
yet	Similar to *'but'*, but used to express a stronger contrast.	**nor**	Similar to *'or'* but used for negatives. *'Was not..., nor was it...'*
for	Means *'because'*. Used in cause-effect statements.		

When using coordinating conjunctions, remember the following.

» *Avoid overusing the conjunction 'and'* – be sure to refer to the previous table and choose a more suitable conjunction for the context.

» *Sentences should not start with coordinating conjunctions* – use discourse markers instead, such as *'Additionally'*, *'Therefore'*, and *'However'*.

» *Use correct punctuation* – provide a comma before the coordinating conjunction.

---

* **Example**

» *Students may have to take an exam. They may also have to write an essay.*

  *Students may have to take an exam, **or** they may have to write an essay.*

» *They could not improve their sales. They were forced to file for bankruptcy.*

  They could not improve their sales, so they were forced to file for bankruptcy.

» *Bill works extremely hard every day to run his company. He also spends time volunteering in the local community.*

  Bill works extremely hard every day to run his company, yet he also spends time volunteering in the local community.

» *The product sales were not strong. They were also not profitable for the company.*

  *The product sales were not strong, **nor** were they profitable for the company.*

» *Airline ticket prices are increasing. The cost of jet fuel is rising.*

  Airline ticket prices are increasing, for the cost of jet fuel is rising.

Subordinate conjunctions

These conjunctions can also be used to combine clauses to form complex sentences. One of these clauses must be a main clause (or *'independent clause'*) and the other a dependent clause. Subordinate conjunctions may be placed between the two clauses, or at the beginning of the first clause. Here is a table of some of the subordinate conjunctions you could use.

after	although	as	because	before
even if	even though	if	provided that	once
rather than	since	so that	than	though
unless	until	when	whenever	whereas
	wherever	while	why	

Subordinate conjunctions are useful for showing a connection or transition that indicates a time, place, or even cause-effect relationships. The structure and punctuation of a subordinate clause is quite important, and often follows one of these formats.

(Main clause) + (subordinate conjunction) + (dependent clause)

(Subordinate conjunction) + (dependent clause) + (,) + (main clause)

Punctuation does become more complicated in some situations, such as the use of relative pronouns like *'who'*, *'which'*, and *'where'* at the start of the dependent clause. In these cases, sometimes you will need a comma, and in other situations, you will not. This depends on the use of essential and non-essential clauses. This book will not go into the complexity of clauses. To learn more, please refer to a grammar textbook for more details.

* Example

» *He was respected by everyone. He worked extremely hard.*

» *He gained everyone's respect **because** he worked extremely hard.*

» *He is going to be late for the meeting. He should contact his colleague.*

» ***Since** he was going to be late to the meeting, he decided to contact his colleague.*

Transitions

Another important consideration for improving cohesion is to tie your ideas together with appropriate transitions so that the reader may read smoothly through your paragraphs and understand the relationship between your ideas. Transitional words or phrases, also known as discourse markers, provided in and between paragraphs, make the whole process of reading more accessible.

Transitions within paragraphs

Here is a paragraph that contains no transitional wording. As you read it, notice the lack of connection from one idea to the next.

> *The company was facing problems with sales. Their store in New York was seeing a reduction in customer numbers over the past year. There is another store in Austin that has also been losing customers for almost 16 months. They made changes to their marketing. Their sales did improve slightly. The sales were still not high enough to make a profit.*

Now take a look at the same paragraph with the inclusion of discourse makers, and a coordinate conjunction. You should notice that sentences now flow cohesively from one idea to the next.

> *The company was facing problems with sales. **First**, their store in New York was seeing a reduction in customer numbers over the past year. **Furthermore**, there is another store in Austin that has also been losing customers for almost 16 months. **Finally**, they made changes to their marketing, **and** sales did improve slightly. **However**, the sales were still not high enough to make a profit.*

To see a table of different discourse markers you could use, and other advice about improving cohesion, please refer to Unit 5.4.

Transitions between paragraphs

Although you do utilise cohesive devices such as **thesis statements**, **topic sentences** and **concluding sentences**, you can further strengthen the cohesion of your essays through the use of transitional words and discourse markers.

Your concluding and topic sentences are great locations for you to strengthen the cohesion in your essay – especially the topic sentences, as the inclusion of a few transitional words (eg *'another'*, *'also'*, and *'finally'*) can offer the reader some narrative. This will aid in highlighting the relationship between paragraphs.

For example, take a look at the following outline of an essay. Notice the use of transitional words in each of the topic sentences, and how these few words help signpost the order of the controlling ideas.

> » *__Thesis statement and essay map__ – ocean pollution has worsened over the past decade. The major contributing factors for this have been the increase in oil spills, corporations' dumping of waste, fly tipping, and cuts to ocean preservation funding.*
>
> » *__Topic sentence 1 – first__, oil spills account for the most significant amount of toxic chemicals in the world's oceans.*
>
> » *__Topic sentence 2__ – corporate waste **also** contributes to ocean pollution in coastal areas.*
>
> » *__Topic sentence 3__ – fly tipping is **another** factor adding to the ever-increasing amount of garbage in our planet's oceans.*
>
> » *__Topic sentence 4 – finally__, some governments have made cuts to the funding of organisations who pioneer the clean-up of our oceans.*

The word *'first'* signals that this is the first idea to be addressed, followed by *'also'* and then *'another'*. There two words emphasise that these ideas are following on from the previous one, and that there is some relationship between these paragraphs. Then, *'finally'* is used to show that the main body of ideas is coming to an end and this is the last idea to be explored.

Summary ✔

Although other areas may need to be revised during the draft writing process, such as the inclusion of more evidence, the points covered in this unit apply to almost every paper. This is especially true after the completion of your first draft, as many students overlook the importance of cohesion and the formation of their sentences. It is great when you finally get all your ideas down on paper, but making it more explicit and accessible to the reader is essential to address when you begin writing your subsequent drafts.

Further reading

For more details about coordinate conjunctions, subordinate conjunctions and discourse markers, check out the following resources:

Bailey, S. (2018) *Academic Writing: A Handbook for International Students*. 5th edn. Abingdon, Oxon: Routledge.

Liss, R. and Davis, J. (2016) *Effective Academic Writing 3: The Researched Essay.* 2nd edn. Oxford: Oxford University Press.

Osmond, A. (2016) *Academic Writing and Grammar for Students.* 2nd edn. London: Sage Publications Ltd.

Swan, M. (2016) *Practical English Usage.* 4th edn. Oxford: Oxford University Press.

11.3 – Proofreading

Keywords

Cliché   A phrase or opinion that is overused and lacks original thought.

Final draft   The final version of your essay, the one you will submit for grading.

Introduction

Once you have reached the **final draft** of your essay, you should look back and check for those common little mistakes that every writer makes. This process is referred to as proofreading your paper, which includes looking for errors surrounding spelling, grammar and punctuation.

Preparation

For proofreading your essay, it may be a good idea to print it out and look at it on paper. Technology can help you proofread, with most word processing software underlining your spelling and grammar mistakes. However, do not rely on these too heavily as they will not identify every error.

Sometimes just looking at your work in a physical form can help you identify mistakes you may overlook while reviewing on a screen. Furthermore, while looking at your essay on paper, you can also write some brief notes or symbols to highlight errors.

Additionally, try to take a break between writing and proofreading your paper. If you decide to proofread immediately after writing, your brain may miss or read over the mistakes you have made. This is because the information is still fresh in your mind. Therefore, you need to spend some time away from your work. One suggestion is to get a good night's sleep before proofreading.

Finally, be prepared to read and re-read your essay. Do not just proofread it once and feel comfortable that you have managed to find every error. If you are being graded on your English, spending a little extra time checking for mistakes could mean the difference between a score of 59 and 60 per cent. It may not be much, but it could be worth it by the end of your course.

Proofreading key

Below is a key of symbols and abbreviations that you may notice your tutors use while reading a draft of your essay. You can use the same while proofreading your work or come up with your own set of symbols and abbreviations. However, remember to keep a key of what they all mean, so you can make the right changes while working on your next draft.

Symbol/ abbreviation	Meaning	Example
T	Tense	*She **studied** in the USA next year.*
VF	Verb form	*He **like** studying in the UK.*
N	Number (*Single/Plural/ Uncountable*)	*He lived in China for two **year**.* *He earns a lot of **moneys**.*
Prep	Preposition	*He lived **on** Spain for two years*
WW	Wrong word	*I like **hearing** to music.*
WF	Word form	*I feel very **happiness**.*
A	Article	*I want to **eat apple**.*
WO	Word order	*I enjoy **to listening** music.*
Sp	Spelling	***Lnodon** is often very cloudy.*
P	Punctuation and capitalisation	*They read many **books.because** they like reading.* ***tokyo** is the capital of **japan**.*
X	Unnecessary word	*It is difficulty to live in **the** today's society.*
//	New paragraph	*In summary, more taxes are **needed. Another** point is that...*
?	Unclear meaning	***Therefore, points are not to the idea of other's suggestions.***

This key should give you an idea of the kinds of errors you should be looking for while proofreading. However, the rest of this unit will cover a few other common mistakes you might encounter.

Pronoun errors

In your essay, you are limited to the kinds of pronouns you can use. As mentioned in Unit 1.2, you should avoid using first- and second-person (eg *'I'*, *'my'*, *'we'*, and *'you'*). However, you may use third-person pronouns in reference to a person or a group (eg a company) you are discussing. When using these kinds of pronouns, you need to be sure they are clearly referring to the correct subject. Take a look at the following example.

> *Both Apple and Microsoft manufacture computers;* **they** *have also had great success at selling smartphones.*

In this sentence, who is the pronoun *'they'* referring to? Does it mean both of them have had success, or just one of them? And if it is only one of them, which one is it? Pronoun errors such as this will confuse your reader and will need to be rewritten to clarify the correct meaning.

> *Both Apple and Microsoft manufacture computers;* **the former** *have also had great success at selling smartphones.*

Misplaced modifiers

Sometimes a modifier is misplaced in your sentences, which results in your reader feeling confused about which word is being modified. Try to place modifiers immediately before or after the word it modifies. For example.

> *When the employees left the office, the managers conducted an inspection.*

What were the managers inspecting? The employees as they left? Or the offices after the employees had left? The modifier *'conducted an inspection'* needs to be placed next to the correct subject.

> *When the employees left, the managers conducted an inspection of the office.*

Dangling modifiers

These usually occur when a sentence, clause or phrase starts with a word ending in *'-ing'* or *'-ed'* and no subject is provided to be modified. You need to inform your reader who or what subject is being modified. Look at the following example of a dangling modifier.

> *The investigation proved to be inconclusive, having not studied the methodology carefully.*

You can see the second clause starts with the word *'having'*. This sentence is unclear in its meaning because there is no subject defined. Did the *'investigation not study the methodology carefully'*? Surely the subject is the person or the group that did the investigation, so an improvement could be.

> **The investigation proved to be inconclusive because the students did not study the methodology carefully.**

Revising wordiness

Sometimes long phrases are used to explain an idea. In academic writing you need to be concise with your language by choosing the right vocabulary. Avoid long and wordy sentences by using specific words or short phrases that get right to the point.

Wordy phrase	Concise alternative
They came to the realisation that...	*They realised that...*
She is of the opinion that...	*She believes that...*
Concerning the matter of...	*About...*
In the event that...	*If...*
In the process of...	*While...*
Regardless of the fact that...	*Although...*
Due to the fact that...	*Because...*

Revising clichés

Those catchy phrases that you may have learnt during high school English classes to make your speech or writing appear natural are actually causing you problems in your academic papers. These clichés are overused, and their impact has become diminished to the point that most readers will find them annoying. Furthermore, they are often quite wordy, when a more concise phrase could be used as an alternative.

Cliché	Alternative
Every coin has two sides	The opposing views are…
A double-edged sword	Has various consequences
Easier said than done	No easy task
Head and shoulders above	Superior to
Last but not least	Lastly
Up in the air	Undecided
Win-win situation	All-round positive outcome

 NOTE: Clichés make you look like a lazy writer who lacks originality. Furthermore, they tend to be quite vague, which can also confuse your reader, especially if they are unfamiliar with the phrase. If you notice any clichés while proofreading, make sure you replace them immediately.

Summary ✔

Proofreading should ideally be used on every draft you write, but must be done before you submit your final draft. You will be constantly making changes with each revision, which means your sentences and paragraphs are always changing. Therefore, a final spelling and grammar check needs to be done to identify any errors that have appeared during your revisions. The key at the beginning of this unit should give you an idea of what to look for, but pay particular attention to the main errors covered in the previous few pages.

Further reading

For more details about the grammar points raised in this unit, check out the following resources:

Bailey, S. (2018) *Academic Writing: A Handbook for International Students*. 5th edn. Abingdon, Oxon: Routledge.

Osmond, A. (2016) *Academic Writing and Grammar for Students*. 2nd edn. London: Sage Publications Ltd.

Swan, M. (2016) *Practical English Usage*. 4th edn. Oxford: Oxford University Press.

11.4 – Writing checklist

Keywords

Marking rubric   Primarily used by teachers to grade assessments. These provide the targets for each criteria and define the difference between pass and fail (and other grade boundaries).

Peer assessment   Working together with a classmate to check each other's work for feedback.

Self-assessment   A process of reviewing and reflecting on your work.

Introduction

Unit 11.1 introduces ways to turn **marking rubrics** into a checklist for **peer and self-assessment**, and this method can be applied to any assignment that supplies you with a rubric. This unit will present a general checklist that can be used with most (but not all) academic papers. Specifically, this checklist is targeted towards argumentative essays.

Essay structure and cohesion

Introduction

» Are your general statements providing relevant background details? *(See Unit 4.1)*

» Does the thesis statement clearly state a claim (*argument*)? *(See Unit 4.2)*

» Is there an essay map given with the thesis statement? Does it include all controlling ideas, and are they in the same order as your main body paragraphs? *(See Unit 4.2)*

Main body paragraphs

» Does every main body paragraph start with a topic sentence? *(See Unit 5.1)*

» Are all the controlling ideas organised logically? *(See Unit 2.3 and 5.1)*

» Are any of the controlling ideas too broad, too narrow, or overlapping with another? *(See Unit 5.1)*

» Are your ideas presented using the SED structure? *(See Unit 5.2)*

» Is there a concluding sentence at the end of each main body paragraph? *(See Unit 5.3)*

Conclusion

» Have you started your conclusion with a summarising discourse marker? *(See Unit 5.4 and 6.1)*

» Did you restate the claim made in your thesis statement? *(See Unit 6.1)*

» Have you provided one or two sentences of summary for each main body paragraph? *(See Unit 6.1)*

» Is there a final idea presented? Is this a clear predication or suggestion that offers more than the statement 'everything will be fine'? *(See Unit 6.2)*

Strength of argument

» Have you provided more than one supporting point for each controlling idea? *(See Unit 5.2)*

» Is each supporting point supported by more than one piece of evidence? *(See Unit 5.2)*

» Have you used a variety of sources? This means, have you used different types of sources? And have you gathered evidence from different authors? *(See Unit 7.1 and 7.4)*

» Do your discussions clearly demonstrate a connection between the evidence and your supporting point? *(See Unit 5.2)*

» Have you provided evidence with your counter-arguments? *(See Unit 3.1)*

» Have you successfully refuted the counter-arguments with a suitable rebuttal? *(See Unit 3.1 and 3.3)*

Use of sources

» Have you checked the reliability of all your sources? Do any of them contain fallacies? *(See Unit 3.3 and 7.4)*

» Do you know who the author is of all sources and what gives them the authority to write about the topic? *(See Unit 7.4)*

» Have you checked your source's details? Have you confirmed any data, numbers and statistics to be correct? *(See Unit 7.4)*

» Have you checked to see if your paraphrases and summaries are indeed your own words? Have you used a search engine or plagiarism checker to confirm this? *(See Unit 9.2 and 9.3)*

» Are all your quotations presented using 'quotation marks'? *(See Unit 9.5)*

» Have you provided citations every time you provide a quotation, paraphrase and summary? *(See Unit 10.2)*

» Is there a reference list entry for every source you have used? Does the author's family name (or organisation) in the citation match the reference list entry? *(See Unit 10.2 and 10.3)*

» Is your reference list consistently formatted using the Harvard referencing style? And has it been provided in alphabetical order? *(See Unit 10.3)*

» If there are any appendix items, have these been referenced in the paper? *(See Unit 12.2)*

Use of English

» Have you proofread for spelling and grammar errors? *(See Unit 11.3)*

» Are there any punctuation errors? Have you also checked your citations and reference list? *(See Unit 10.2 and 10.3)*

» Is the vocabulary and grammar used complex and concise? Are there any parts of the essay that sound like spoken language? *(See Unit 1.2)*

» Are there any first- or second-person pronouns? *(See Unit 1.2)*

» Have you used any reporting verbs to introduce your evidence? *(See Unit 9.6)*

» Does the essay use transitional words or discourse makers to improve cohesion? *(See Unit 11.2)*

» Are there any clichés or wordy statements that need to be removed from the essay? *(See Unit 11.3)*

» Have you noticed any misplaced or dangling modifiers? *(See Unit 11.3)*

Formatting

» Is your essay formatted appropriately? Does it look tidy and professional? *(See Unit 12.1)*

» If you tutor has asked for a cover page, is it correctly formatted and does it include relevant details? *(See Unit 12.2)*

» Have you included all necessary items in your appendices? Have these items been referenced in the main body of your essay? *(See Unit 12.2)*

Summary ✔

This checklist will help you to peer and self-assess your essays, but you should still pay close attention to the requirements in the marking rubric. There will sometimes be criteria that are not covered by any of the questions on this checklist. Therefore, you will need to create some of your own questions using the method outlined in Unit 11.1.

Unit 12 Formatting

12.1 – Margins, font and spacing

Keywords

Assignment brief A document outlining details such as: the assessment task, deadlines, and how the work will be graded.

Introduction

When submitting an essay for grading, you should aim to present your paper in a clean and professional manner. Most colleges and universities have their own formatting rules that you may be required to follow, and these are often provided to you in your student handbook or your **assignment briefs**. However, this unit will provide you with some general formatting rules you could use for your margins, font choices and line spacing.

Location of settings

As there are several software packages available for word processing (e.g. Microsoft Word, Apple Pages, Open Office, and Libre Office), providing directions to the location of relevant settings would be rather difficult to achieve. Additionally, this is complicated further by the fact that these software packages are constantly being updated, resulting in some settings being moved from one location to another.

Therefore, to aid you in your search for these settings, it is recommended that you use the help function built into your word processor (or by doing a quick search online). For example, if you want to edit the space around the edge of your page, in the help search bar type in the word 'margins'.

Page margins

The page margin is the space left around the edge of your essay. If it is too big, it will reduce how many words you can fit on to one page. However, if it is too small, it may cause printing issues (should you need to provide a paper copy). Furthermore, when printing out your essay, the margins allow for you and your tutors to make notes on feedback.

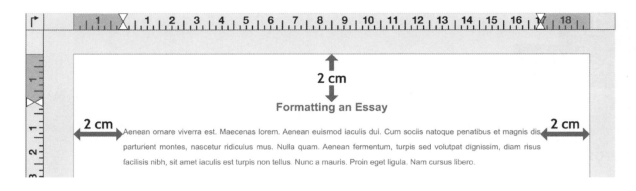

Margin Settings			
Top:	2 cm	**Bottom:**	2 cm
Left:	2 cm	**Right:**	2 cm

Header and footer

In the margins at the top and bottom of your page, you should provide some details about the assignment and who wrote the essay. In the header (the top margin), you should include the name of the module on the left, and the assignment name on the right.

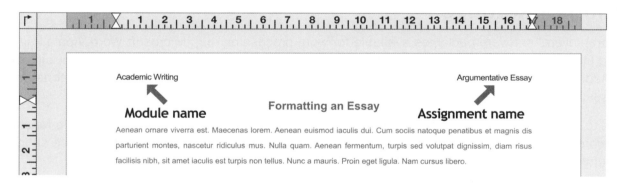

Then, in the footer (bottom margin), you should include your name or student ID number on the left, and the page numbers on the right.

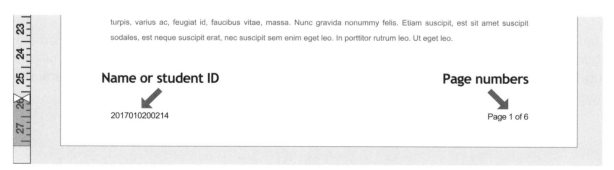

Font choice, size and formatting

You should aim to use a clean and easy-to-read font. Be consistent throughout your essay; do not have font changes across sentences or paragraphs. To ensure all text is the same, once you have completed your essay, select all your text and chose a font from the drop-down menu (usually located on the toolbar or sidebar).

Following is a list of suitable fonts that are clean, professional and easy to read (on the left), and fonts that are difficult to read or unnecessarily styled (on the right).

Acceptable fonts	Unacceptable fonts
Arial	**Arial Black**
Calibri	Comic Sans MS
Georgia	Courier New
Helvetica	**Impact**
Times New Roman	*Lucida Handwriting*

Throughout your paper, use reasonable font sizes that allow you to make the most out of each page. Do not use larger font sizes to make it look like you have written more. Try to stick to the following guidelines.

Section	Size	Formatting	Alignment
Title	12 pt	**B** *I* U	
Headings and sub-headings	11 pt	**B** *I* U	
Body text	11 pt	None	

Line spacing

You should include a space between each line of text, and an even larger space between each paragraph. As with the formatting of your fonts, different parts of your essay have their own line spacing format. Once you navigated to the settings, use the following guidelines.

Section	Before	After	Line spacing
Title	1 line	0 line	1.5 lines
Headings and sub-headings	1 line	0 line	1.5 lines
Body text	0 line	1 line	1.5 lines

 NOTE: Some tutors may request your line spacing to be two lines throughout the entire paper. This allows suitable space for tutors to write feedback between each line of text (on a printed version). Remember to check your assignment brief and follow any formatting rules outlined in their rules and guidelines.

Reference list

Line spacing settings for the reference list are slightly different, and you are also required to make changes to the indentation settings too (these are found in the same location as the line spacing settings). Here are the guidelines you should use for your reference list.

Indentation			
Left	**Right**	**Special**	**By**
0 mm	0 mm	Handing	2 ch
Spacing			
Before	**After**	**Line spacing**	
0 line	1 line	Single	

Summary ✔

Formatting is something that many students overlook but it is actually quite important. Sometimes you may even be graded on the presentation of your work, so you should always aim to produce papers that look tidy and professional. Editing the margins, fonts and line spacing allows you to get as much information onto each page as possible without bunching everything together. The spaces you leave are essential for the reader to feel comfortable while reading your work, as well as allowing for room to make notes.

12.2 – Cover page and appendices

Keywords

Appendices	A section provided at the end of a piece of work to provide further details that do not belong the body of the work, such as charts and questionnaires. A single entry is called an *Appendix*.
Assignment brief	A document outlining details such as: the assessment task, deadlines, and how the work will be graded.
Footer	Part of formatting your documents. Located at the very bottom of the page, providing details on the writer and page numbers.
Header	Part of formatting your documents. Located at the very top of the page, providing details on module name and assessment title.
ID number	An identification number, often provided to students when they enrol at university.

Introduction

Two areas that have not been discussed throughout the book are the cover page and appendices. The former appears at the very start of your paper, and the latter comes at the very end. The cover page provides some necessary details in the same way a book cover would, and the appendices are there to present the non-essential information that supports your work but does not belong in the main body.

Cover page

On the cover page, you will inform your reader of a few basic but essential details about you and your assignment. Make sure to include the following.

» The title of your paper.

» Your name and/or your student ID number.

» Module name.

» Module tutor's name.

» Name of college/university.

» Date of deadline.

 NOTE: It is worth checking the **assignment brief**, or asking your tutor, if any further details are required. Furthermore, not every assignment will need you to supply a cover page, especially for shorter papers of around three or four pages.

Font, font size and formatting

The choice of font for your cover page should match the font you have chosen to use in the main body of your paper. Therefore, if your essay is written using 'Arial', make sure your cover page also uses the same. Here is a table of settings you can use for formatting the different sections of your cover page.

Section	Size	Formatting	Alignment
Title	12 pt	**B** *I* U̲	
Your name and/or student ID	12 pt	None	
Module details, college/ university, and deadline	12 pt	None	

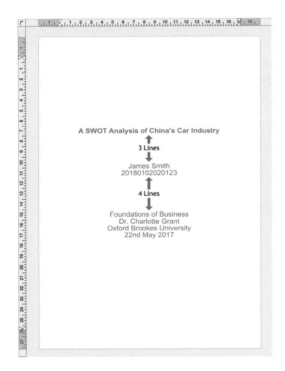

Page layout

The details on the cover page should be located in the centre of the page, with a suitable number of lines between each section. To the left is an example of how your cover page should be presented.

Header and footer

In the main body of your paper, you are required to provide details in the header and footer of your page (see Unit 12.1). However, since most of these details are provided on the cover page, there is no need to repeat this information in a header and footer.

Therefore, you will need to turn off header and footers for the first page of your document.

Appendices

This section can be titled either the *'Appendix'* (only one item) or *'Appendices'* (more than one item). Here you can provide your readers with non-essential information that is relevant in supporting your paper, but does not belong in the main body. This could include items such as the following.

» Calculations used to reach an answer (useful for mathematical and scientific subjects).

» Visual data (eg graphs, charts, tables, figures, diagrams).

» Photographs, screenshots (eg from videos or games), drawings, and maps.

» Correspondence (eg emails and letters).

» Transcripts of face to face, online, and over the phone interviews.

» Questionnaires or surveys used to collect data (ie collection method for primary research).

» Large sections of articles that are too long to be presented as a quotation.

Referencing your appendices

Appendices are presented at the end of your paper to avoid breaking up the cohesion of your ideas. If you were to provide any of the items above in the middle of your essay, it would distract the reader or even cause them to lose the connection between one paragraph and the next.

Therefore, if you need to refer to any of these items in your main body, you will need to provide a citation. However, this is not a citation used to refer to a book or website; this is to reference the appendix item at the end of your paper. You can cite your appendix items using one of the following formats.

> *The final results **(see Appendix 3)** clearly show an increased trend towards...*
> *An example of the questionnaire can be found in **Appendix C**...*

NOTE: You can identify each appendix item using either numbers or letters (starting at '1' or 'A'), but make sure you are consistent and use the same method throughout your entire paper.

Presenting your appendices

Your appendices should come after your reference list; each appendix item should be given its own page and provided in the same order as they are referenced in the main body (eg *Appendix 1*, *Appendix 2*, and then *Appendix 3*). At the top of each page, correctly label each item using the heading settings from Unit 12.1.

Appendix example

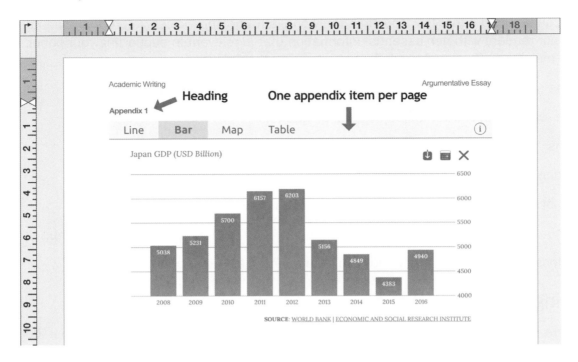

Summary ✔

Both cover pages and appendices are not required for every assignment. However, when they are, they do need to be presented logically, especially the appendices. You need to remember to reference each appendix item in your paper, and then present each corresponding item in the correct order at the very end of your paper. As with all formatting guidelines mentioned throughout this set of units, it is recommended that you check your student handbook and assignment briefs for any further requirements.

Exercises

1.2 – Features of academic writing

Exercise 1

ⓘ Choose the most appropriate word for use in academic writing.

a. The company has made **substantial/huge** changes in its approach to marketing.

b. **Lots of/numerous** attempts have been made to find a relationship between the two **big/major** contributing factors.

c. First impressions are **extremely/really** important.

d. A rise in unemployment is just one of the **consequences/things** that will happen with the introduction of automated production lines.

Exercise 2

ⓘ Match the following verbs with their corresponding nouns.

Analyse	Deduction
Deduce	Rejection
Illustrate	Analysis
Indicate	Progression
Invest	Revision
Implicate	Illustration
Progress	Indication
Reject	Investment
Revise	Suggestion
Suggest	Implication

Exercise 3

ⓘ Rewrite the following sentences into a nominalised form, by identifying the relevant verb and replacing it with its noun form. An example has been provided.

> *The company's value was **decreasing** rapidly, and investors **were becoming concerned**.*
>
> *The rapid **decrease** in the company's value was causing **concern** for investors.*

a. The data enables scientists to formulate precise predictions.

....

b. The students researched the topic but uncovered no relevant evidence.

....

c. Candidates need to impress the employers during an interview.

....

Exercise 4

ⓘ Replace the word in brackets with a more formal word or phrase.

a. Officials are in the process of organising a (**get together**)................................... to discuss potential strategies.

b. Staff members who breach their contract will be (**given the sack**) ....

c. A country's economy is affected by (**things**)................................... such as population, natural resources and infrastructure.

d. Therefore, the company's future is likely to be (**nice**) ....

Exercise 5

ⓘ Read the following two paragraphs and decide which is more objective.

a. Apple's App Store provides users with access to over 2.2 million apps (Statista, 2018), which generates $26.5 billion (USD) for its developers (Leswing, 2018). Each app has to go through a rigorous review process to determine if they are suitable for its users. Issues that Apple will monitor for are: system crashes, user interface errors, misleading information, and malicious files that affect its users' security (Apple, no date).

b. The App Store, available on all Apple devices, may be a lucrative business opportunity for app developers. However, the review process that Apple subjects every submission to is ridiculously strict, meaning many apps are often rejected. Google's Play Store is far friendlier to its developers, allowing more creative freedom while still providing a great source of income.

Exercise 6

ⓘ Suggest improvements for the following sentences by avoiding the use of 'you' and 'we'.

a. In the following section, we will introduce the potential consequences.

....

b. You can increase productivity by taking regular breaks.

....

c. We gathered research by conducting interviews with the general public.

....

d. You should take note of the suggestions outlined in this textbook.

....

Exercise 7

ⓘ Read the following sentence pairs and identify when hedging has been used.

a. It may be said that the commitments to fighting global warming are becoming less important than five years ago.

The commitments to fighting global warming are now less important than five years ago.

b. The anti-vaccination movement has caused an outbreak in many diseases among children in the US.

The increased cases of childhood diseases could be the result of the recent anti-vaccination movement sweeping across the US.

c. Perhaps the internet is to blame for plagiarism becoming more prevalent in university assignments.

The internet is clearly a plagiarist's key resource, and its popularity is the reason why plagiarism is more commonly detected in university assignments.

English for Academic Purposes: A Handbook for Students

2.1 – Understanding assessment tasks

Exercise 1

ℹ Using the example of a marking rubric, answer the following questions.

a. In which criteria will your use of SED structure be graded?

....

b. For 'Structure', what is the difference between a distinction and a merit?

....

c. If you scored 55% for 'Use of evidence', what could you have done to raise the score to a merit?

....

d. For 'Spelling and grammar', what is the difference between a pass and a fail?

....

Criteria	Distinction (70–100%)	Merit (60–69%)	Pass (40–59%)	Fail (0–39%)
Structure (30%)	Develops all ideas using SED structure. Logically connects paragraphs.	SED structure has been used in every paragraph, but not for every idea.	SED structure has been used in some paragraphs.	SED structure has rarely, or never, been used.
Use of evidence (30%)	All ideas presented with at least two pieces of evidence. Counter-arguments have always been provided.	Majority of ideas utilise at least two pieces of evidence. At least one counter-argument per paragraph.	Provides evidence with ideas but relies heavily on quotations. Counter-arguments have at least been attempted.	Evidence not always provided or is just quotations. Counter-arguments have not been attempted.

Criteria	Distinction (70–100%)	Merit (60–69%)	Pass (40–59%)	Fail (0–39%)
Language (20%)	Formal and complex language has been used throughout. Provides a balance of varied sentences.	Formal language has been used throughout. Noticeable use of basic word forms.	Attempts at using formal language, with noticeable colloquial words/ phrases.	Excessive use of informal language. Sentences are repetitive in both form and vocabulary.
Spelling and grammar (20%)	Essay is essentially error-free. No noticeable spelling or grammar mistakes.	Minor errors in spelling or grammar. Does not impede understanding.	Frequent errors that distract the reader. Overall meaning can be comprehended.	Numerous errors that seriously impede understanding.

Exercise 2

ⓘ Read the following assessment task and identify the task and subject/focus words.

Social media has become an essential communication tool for most major companies. However, its use can be both beneficial and detrimental. Evaluate the consequences that companies may face by having a social media presence.

2.2 – Creating new ideas

Exercise 1

ⓘ Look at the example of a linear brainstorm created for an essay with the title of *'cutting down on litter'*. Use the following information to create a mind map version of these notes in the space provided.

Cutting down on litter - Brainstorm

Introduction:	Solutions:	Problems:	Way forward:
> Purpose of report	> Punishment: fines	> Cause: laziness	> What?
> What is in the report	> Education: schools	> Cause: ignorance	> How?
Conclusion:	> Education: workplaces	> Cause: pests	> When?
> Summary	> Incentives: rewards	> Cause: smells	> Who?
> Recommendations		> Cause: disease	

2.3 – Planning an academic paper

Exercise 1

ℹ First, read the following assessment task.

When students attend university, they develop in many different ways. Their attitude, personality traits and habits are all affected by this move from high school into higher education. Illustrate three ways in which students change while studying at university.

a. Identify the task and subject/focus words.

b. Brainstorm some ideas relating to this topic. This can be done as either linear notes or a mind map.

NOTE: In order to have enough space for your brainstorm, you will need to complete this stage of the exercise in your notebook or on a separate piece of paper.

c. Look at your brainstorm. Rewrite three of these ideas as complete sentences.

1.

....

2.

....

3.

....

d. For each of the three ideas above, write down an example.

1.

....

2.

....

3.

....

English for Academic Purposes: A Handbook for Students

e. Using the information above, complete the following table.

Idea	Example	What is the connection?
1)		
2)		
3)		

f. Write down a suitable thesis statement based on the details provided in the assessment task.

....

....

....

g. Write down your three ideas (not including the examples) into one complete sentence.

....

....

....

h. Think about how you would start this essay. Write down a few general ideas that could be used to introduce your reader to this topic.

....

....

....

Now, using your answers to the previous questions, complete the outline below. Do not simply copy your answers, but instead try to paraphrase your ideas. Furthermore, you may need to add some extra detail.

NOTE: The letter after each heading corresponds to one of the questions above. For example, under '*Supporting point (c – 1)*', write down the first answer given to question **c**):

Introduction
General statements (h):
Thesis statement (f):
Essay map (g):

Body paragraph 1
Supporting point (c – 1):
Evidence/example (d – 1):
Discussion (e – 1 – connection):

Body paragraph 2
Supporting point (c – 2):
Evidence/example (d – 2):

Discussion (e – 2 – connection):

Body paragraph 3

Supporting point (c – 3):

Evidence/example (d – 3):

Discussion (e – 3 – connection):

3.1 – Arguments in writing

Exercise 1

ⓘ Decide if the following arguments have been formed using deductive or inductive reasoning.

a. To study for a master's degree, students must have a minimum 2:1 classification. As Sarah achieved a 2:1, she will be able to study for a master's.

b. 50 per cent of students who attend this university receive government grants. Therefore, it is likely that half of all students who attend university receive government grants.

c. The tourism industry was left devastated by the 2008 financial crisis. Consequently, investments in hotels and restaurants are a somewhat high risk.

d. Companies have repeatedly stated they are looking for recent graduates with strong public speaking skills. As a result, many universities now require students to complete at least one presentation assessment across all courses.

Exercise 2

ⓘ Label the three deductive arguments with one of the following labels.

Valid and sound	Invalid, but with true premises	Valid, but with untrue premises

a. It has been reported that Apple is currently developing a car. Their biggest competition may be Tesla, who have been producing cars since their formation. Therefore, both Apple and Tesla can be labelled as automotive companies.

....

b. All countries that take part in the Eurovision Song Contest are located in the continent of Europe. Australia is one of the countries to participate in the contest. So, Australia can be considered as a European country.

....

English for Academic Purposes: A Handbook for Students

c. Sir Edmund Hillary climbed to the summit of Mount Everest in 1953. There are no previously recorded or confirmed attempts at reaching the summit before this date. Therefore, Sir Edmund Hillary rightfully holds the title of 'the first man to climb Everest'.

....

3.3 – Identifying fallacies

Exercise 1

ⓘ Match the types of fallacies listed in the following table with the following examples.

Appeal to emotion	Fallacy of induction
Fallacy of clarity	Argument against the source

a. Greenpeace awarded the company an environmentally friendly score of 8.9, which is higher than any of their competitors. It is clear that every product they produce is helping to save the environment.

....

b. Properties in school neighbourhoods should only be sold to families. This needs to be done to ensure the safety of the children attending the school.

....

c. The organisation's leader only just managed to graduate from high school, and now he has somehow managed to work his way into a management role. He clearly has no idea if these reforms will return positive results.

....

d. Two wrongs do not make a right, but three lefts do make a right.

....

4.1 – General statements

Exercise 1

ℹ For each essay topic, read the two suggested opening sentences and decide which is a more suitable hook to grab the reader's attention. Give reasons for your choice.

a. Topic: The future of print media

» With the development of technology, print media has struggled to attract strong audience numbers.

» The notion that print media is on its way to becoming extinct may be an overstatement.

....

....

....

b. Topic: Investing in cryptocurrencies

» Cryptocurrencies are now more popular than ever and will replace the traditional banking systems.

» Originally used as form of payment on the black market, cryptocurrencies have now grown in popularity among mainstream users (Foley, Karlsen and Putninš, 2018).

....

....

....

c. Topic: The importance of human resource departments

» In 2014, Netflix sent shockwaves through the business world by essentially reinventing the human resource department (McCord, 2014).

» In the business world, a common question is 'Why are human resource departments so important?'.

....

....

....

Exercise 2

ⓘ Decide the correct order of the following sentences (from general to specific), and then draw a line connecting each sentence together (starting from the hook and finishing with the thesis statement).

However, think carefully about the path your line will take. You are not allowed to let any lines between sentences cross each other.

However, cultural differences have also hampered some deals and even caused partnerships to dissolve.

Since the early 1990s, international trade has expanded exponentially.

Uber, the ride-sharing app, has failed to develop their business with international partners due to their strong American approach to business.

Furthermore, many developing countries have benefited greatly from international trade, causing their GDP to increase rapidly.

Therefore, companies need to successfully navigate their foreign partner's differences by developing an understanding of their cultural characteristics.

This has allowed for cross-cultural influences on business practices, many of which have had positive impacts.

Exercise 3

ℹ Arrange the following sentences into the correct order (from general to specific).

Introduction 1

a. Tech companies such as Apple and Samsung have taken notice of these concerns and decided to address them through the use of wearables.

b. The millennial generation places health and fitness high on their list of concerns.

c. However, this data can be misleading and inaccurate, leading to users potentially risking their well-being.

d. Notably, smartwatches have enabled users to track their health through collecting data such as heart rate levels, exercise metrics and calorie counting.

e. They are especially interested in the amount of time spent exercising and keeping track of their nutritional intake.

Introduction 2

a. Furthermore, one report suggests that the US is subjected to a mass shooting, on average, every 64 days (Cohen, Azreal and Miller, 2014).

b. This move proved to be successful, as 22 years later, gun-related massacres are a very rare occurrence across the country.

c. Based on this example, questions are often raised as to why the United States does not take the same action.

d. In 1996, Australia drafted a law banning all automatic and military-style weapons in a bid to eradicate mass shootings.

a. These statistics highlight the importance of change, and that it is now time that the US takes action to restrict access to firearms.

Exercise 4

ⓘ Write down a selection of general statements that could be used to introduce a topic surrounding the *'effects of tourism development'*.

....

....

....

....

....

4.2 – Thesis statements and essay maps

Exercise 1

ⓘ Identify which one of the following thesis statements provides the reader with a clear claim. For the other four, write down why these are poor examples of thesis statements.

a. The government is telling lies about the so-called effects of global warming.

....

b. Global warming is bad.

....

c. This essay will discuss global warming.

....

d. Global warming has contributed heavily to recent unpredictable weather patterns.

....

e. Global warming is an issue that must be solved.

....

Exercise 2

ⓘ Rewrite the following thesis statements. Be sure to provide a claim that is specific and can be realistically supported.

a. Children watch too much TV.

....

....

b. American universities can be improved.

....

....

c. Urbanisation has negative effects.

....

....

Exercise 3

🛈 Attempt to write your own thesis statement based on the following topics.

a. Topic: Alcoholism

....

....

b. Topic: Animal testing

....

....

c. Topic: Renewable energy sources

....

....

Exercise 4

🛈 Read the following thesis statements. Then, using the list of controlling ideas, write an essay map combining all three ideas into one complete sentence.

a. Thesis statement: The most effective way to reduce the homeless population is to provide access to essential services.

Controlling ideas: 1) Food banks, 2) Public restrooms/showers, 3) Shelters

....

....

b. **Thesis statement:** As smoking is a toxic and life-threatening habit, restrictions need to be enforced.

Controlling ideas: 1) Limiting access, 2) Raising prices, 3) Public smoking

....

....

c. **Thesis statement:** Education systems are becoming overly dependent on technology, leading to students lacking the ability to think independently.

Controlling ideas: 1) Mood disorders, 2) Poor memory, 3) Social skills

....

....

5.1 – Topic sentences

Exercise 1

ℹ️ Identify the topic and controlling idea in the following topic sentences.

    a. To be an effective group member requires excellent communication skills.

    b. All potential risks need evaluating before any investment decision.

    c. Lowering the drinking age limit will have noticeable effects on crime rates.

    d. Identity fraud is one of the most significant threats to the online shoppers.

Exercise 2

ℹ️ Using the same example thesis statement, essay map and topic sentence provided in Unit 5.1 (repeated below), write a topic sentence for both paragraphs 2 and 3.

Thesis statement and essay map: Children's social interactions have been negatively affected by the increased use of technologies such as smartphones and tablets. Their attitude towards family members, their peers and even strangers, has become increasingly disrespectful or even violent.

Paragraph 1 – Topic sentence: Many family relationships have suffered a breakdown due to their children's increased access to technology.

Paragraph 2 – Topic sentence

....

....

....

Paragraph 3 – Topic sentence

....

....

....

Exercise 3

ⓘ Read the following paragraph, and identify what the controlling idea may be.

Improving employee motivation
An annual appraisal process can highlight the opportunities for progression. Young (2014) found that when employees reflect on where they are now, and what steps need to be taken for promotion, their overall efficiency begins to improve. Even if realistically there are no positions available in the immediate future, employees still recognise that they need to show their worth if they are to be considered when a position becomes available (Smith, 2016). Furthermore, providing training to develop employees can also aid in raising staff morale. Training can take the form of in-house workshops (Ryan, 2011) or via offering recognised qualifications such as NVQs (Jones, 2015). This portrays the idea that management values their employees enough to develop their abilities, rather than merely dismissing staff once they reach a level of incompetence. These opportunities motivate employees far beyond a simple salary increase or bonus payment ever could. Additionally, they can be even more effective when provided alongside a robust set of benefits.

a. What are some potential keywords that could be used to describe the controlling idea of this paragraph?

....

....

....

b. Choose one of the keywords listed above to write a suitable topic sentence.

....

....

....

Exercise 1

ⓘ Using SED structure, identify if the following sentences are providing supporting points, evidence or discussions. Then, create two short paragraphs by putting the sentences in the correct order.

a. Attempts may be made to provide stimulation, in the hope that the animals will be put at ease. However, their well-being is overshadowed by the primary goal of entertaining the ever-growing number of guests and increasing profits.

b. The possibility of civil war breaking out in countries such as the UK or US is highly unlikely.

c. This is especially the case in zoos, where the artificial surroundings heighten stress levels among the animals.

d. Although both countries do face economic challenges at times, they are often able to quickly recover. Furthermore, their populations are extremely diverse with many citizens from the majority of the world's nations.

e. This is because these countries do have the two main characteristics often associated with the outbreak of civil war, which are an underdeveloped economy, and a general population that is lacking in diversity.

f. Animals kept in captivity are subjected to unrealistic and cruel environmental conditions.

NOTE: Citations have been removed from any sentences providing evidence. This has been done to challenge your ability in judging the context of the sentences.

Exercise 2

ⓘ Create a main body paragraph by putting the following sentences into the correct order. Use the SED structure to aid in your decision-making.

a. By coaching students and providing small achievable goals, the tutor should be able to raise the student's self-belief in their abilities (Zepke and Leach, 2010).

b. First, it is crucial to understand if students are aiming to digest as much knowledge as possible or do the bare minimum to pass.

c. Therefore, it is essential for teachers to foster or encourage an in-depth approach to learning to raise motivational levels.

d. Once students shift away from a surface approach towards in-depth learning, the next step is to encourage an inclusive learning environment.

e. Understanding a student's approach to learning is key to ensuring that they are genuinely benefitting from their education.

f. Biggs and Tang (2011) categorised two approaches to learning, which are known as a 'surface' or 'deep' approach.

g. Through this method, the students become more engaged in the classroom and with the subject itself.

h. The surface approach is often adopted by students who are not internally motivated to study, taking on a university course due to social or family pressure.

Exercise 3

ⓘ Choose the most suitable piece of evidence to use alongside the following supporting point.

Supporting point: The perceived high quality of British higher education attracts numerous international students every year.

Evidence 1: About 20% of overseas students who applied to UK universities in 2015 applied to study at Nottingham University, and since then the number has grown (Chen, 2017).

Evidence 2: More and more students study abroad, and the UK is one of the most popular destinations.

Evidence 3: Research conducted by the Harvard Graduate School of Education (2017) revealed that since 2015 there has been a significant increase in the number of students from Asia and the Middle East choosing to study their undergraduate degrees at UK universities

Once you have chosen which evidence is most suitable, write a discussion to connect the details provided in the evidence with the supporting point provided.

....

....

....

....

5.3 – Concluding sentences

Exercise 1

ⓘ Read the following paragraphs, and the thesis statement of the paragraph that should follow. From this, write a suitable concluding sentence to summarise and link these paragraphs together.

Paragraph 1: *Several internal factors are to blame for the UK's current housing crisis. Britain's rising population is possibly the most significant contributor to this shortage of homes. In the past ten years, the UK's population has risen by over two million (DNS, 2015). Consequently, this rapid increase coupled with the lack of investment in the construction of new accommodation (Business View, 2016) has resulted in the value of current properties reaching levels that many cannot afford to buy or rent.*

Paragraph 2: *The housing crisis has been further influenced by overseas investors...*

Concluding sentence

....

....

....

Paragraph 1: *Social media sites have facilitated the practice of cyberbullying, especially among teenagers, who post details of their every action. Davis (2016) found that teenagers feel as if they have 'no choice' in 'demonstrating they have an active life' to their friends. However, this places them in the spotlight and allows for others to identify situations that can lead to ridicule. One poorly framed picture could lead to unfavourable comments regarding their appearance. 'I ended up dropping out of school!' exclaimed Sarah, 'a simple photo of me enjoying my holiday led to months of hurtful comments regarding my weight' (Davis, 2016). In the past, it was only celebrities who would receive negative comments regarding the unflattering photos captured by paparazzi. Nowadays, thanks to social media, teenagers are subjecting themselves to the same treatment due to their desire to demonstrate to all that they live an active and exciting lifestyle.*

Paragraph 2: *Misleading and untruthful news stories have also gained in popularity thanks to social media platforms...*

Concluding sentence

....

....

....

5.4 – Cohesion

Exercise 1

ℹ Decide which of the discourse markers in the following table are suitable for connecting the following sentences together. **NOTE:** You may only use each discourse marker once.

Admittedly	Alternatively	Generally	In conclusion
In other words	Similarly	Subsequently	Therefore

a. As of 2017, companies such as BMW, Jaguar and VW can be found parked up next to Tesla in the charging bays of your local car park. ...., electric vehicles are here to stay.

b. Upcoming regulations will restrict the sale of coal. ...., many agencies are responding to this by developing alternatives, such as 'clean coal' variants.

c. Based on this experiment, the results showed a 74% increase in the amount of gases released.., due to some contaminations, the experiment may not have produced an accurate set of results.

d. Jones (2014) proposed a drastic overhaul of all written assessments within the university. ...., Smith (2015) commented that assessments in their current form were unacceptable and needed updating.

e. Those customers who were unhappy with the final product had the option of downgrading to the previous version. ...., customers were also provided with a refund option.

f. Finally, due to localising the advertisements, the Asian market saw a tenfold increase in product sales. ...., by merely making a few adjustments to the marketing material for each region, an apparent increase in sales can be achieved.

g. In March of 2016, the administration announced they would soon call for a public vote on the matter. ...., in the following month, the vote took place and the results did not allow for the law to pass.

h. The cost of the insurance policy will increase proportionately with the expansion of the grounds. ...., this implies that as the buildings are erected, the potential pay-out by the insurer is likely to be higher.

6.1 – Elements of a conclusion

Exercise 1

ⓘ First, examine the following essay outline. Pay attention to the claim being made in the thesis statement, the controlling idea of each paragraph, and ideas for supporting points.

Introduction

Thesis statement: a prevention over punishment approach is the most effective way to tackle the growing number of young offenders.

Main body paragraph 1

Topic sentence: provide after-school programmes to engage youths with education.

Supporting point 1: sports teams and games

Supporting point 2: creative classes (e.g. art, music, and drama)

Main body paragraph 2

Topic sentence: work experience will distract teens from committing crimes.

Supporting point 1: internships at local and professional organisations

Supporting point 2: volunteer activities

Main body paragraph 3

Topic sentence: help teens avoid poor life decisions with a health-based curriculum.

Supporting point 1: workshops about the harmful effects of alcohol

Supporting point 2: dealing with stress and social pressures

Now decide which of the following conclusion paragraphs would be most suitable for this essay. Give reasons for your decision.

a. As the saying goes, prevention is better than the cure – or in this case, better than punishment. Teenagers can be convinced to behave better if enough people and organisations get involved. Schools, businesses and local communities can all pull together to offer services that distract these youths from their anti-social activities. The punishment route has been tried and tested, and it is not working. Therefore, the way forward is to invest in more supportive and constructive options.

b. In conclusion, reaching out and offering support to local teenagers is far more effective than handing out punishments. By establishing after-school programmes, such as football clubs or music lessons, teenagers are offered a chance to participate in activities they enjoy while remaining in an educational environment. Furthermore, local businesses can provide internships to help keep the youths stimulated while earning a little income as a bonus. Alternatively, local communities can also provide volunteer work that helps these teens gain experience and see the effects of being a positive member of society versus a negative influence. Finally, many youths make poor decisions due to a lack of education, especially regarding alcohol abuse. Sometimes this is caused due to peer pressure or dealing with the stress that puberty places on a youth approaching adulthood. Through implementing these prevention methods, the number of youth gangs on our neighbourhood's streets will decrease, and the teenagers themselves will be provided with a positive future ahead.

....

....

....

c. In summary, prevention over a punishment approach is undoubtedly the most effective way to tackle a large number of young offenders. Although punishment is useful to some extent, many teens will merely re-offend. Schools need to step in and provide their students with after-school programmes, such as sports teams, art classes, music lessons or drama clubs. Because teenagers find these activities far more interesting than maths, science and English, they will gain a favourable impression of school if they participate in these programmes while in a school environment. Additionally, businesses in the local community could provide some exciting internships, especially those who are professional and well-established organisations. This is because if teens are going to take on a part-time job, it must be with the best companies. Plus, they will earn a little income while doing so. However, even volunteer work would be another option, but as this is 'free' work, and can be perceived as possibly boring, the chances of success for this initiative are slim. Finally, to help teens avoid making poor life decisions, education can be provided regarding health and well-being. Explaining the adverse effects of alcohol will aid in reducing cases of underage drinking. Moreover, services that help teens through the challenges they are facing, such as puberty, can further improve their understanding of how to deal with social pressures that may lead to stress and self-harm. Surely this is worth experimenting with, and if nothing changes or the results are inconclusive, then the punishment option is always there as a backup option.

....

....

....

6.2 – Final ideas

Exercise 1

❶ Identify if the following sentences are presenting a prediction, suggestion, or neither.

a. At this stage, it is entirely up to the local governments to deter the gentrification of neighbourhoods by investing in the construction of middle-income housing.

....

b. The points raised in this essay should give some pause for thought, and hopefully lead to a more favourable outcome for all.

....

c. The time for issuing warnings has passed, and it is now up to every individual to make lifestyle changes if the environment is to have any chance of recovering from the damages caused by excessive pollution.

....

d. As electric cars increase in popularity, the major oil companies will begin to shift their interests elsewhere, with renewable energy being the most attractive investment.

....

e. It is clear to see that security cameras pose no threat to the general population's privacy and that only criminals, or those who have committed terrible deeds, should be fearful of being watched.

....

f. Although some iOS applications have already begun to utilise the subscription model to increase revenue, this is undoubtedly going to be more common across all platforms within the next five years.

....

7.1 – Types of sources

Exercise 1

ⓘ For each of the following types of sources, provide a list of advantages and disadvantages.

Type of source	Advantages	Disadvantages
Book/e-book		
Journals/ e-journals		
Newspapers		
Magazines		
Websites		
Online videos		

7.2 – Types of evidence

Exercise 1

ℹ Label the following pieces of evidence as *'facts'*, *'opinions'*, *'statistics'*, *'quotations'*, or *'examples'*.

a. Apple released the iPod on 23 October 2001.

b. Italian food is the easiest and most enjoyable food to prepare.

c. Margaret Thatcher was the first female Prime Minister in the UK.

d. In one experiment, only 1.2% of 98,188 hard drives suffered a failure.

e. Starbucks is just one of many coffee chains still using non-recyclable cups.

f. Online shopping is always cheaper than buying from a physical store.

g. In the music industry, digital revenues increased by US$9.4bn during 2017.

h. The more money a company has, the more successful they will be.

i. Yates suggests the current regulations *'need to be relaxed'*.

j. Methods, such as SWOT, can be utilised to assess businesses thoroughly.

k. Only 38% of adults over 75 years old are considered to be physically active.

l. *'It is important never to put design before function'*, says Williamson.

m. One kilogram of lemons contains more sugar than one kilogram of strawberries.

n. Taylor stresses that *'progression is steady'*, but *'difficulties do lie ahead'*.

o. The hotel should invest in developing its facilities, perhaps by adding a fitness centre.

7.3 – Conducting research

Exercise 1

ⓘ Start by looking at the essay topic below.

Discuss opportunities or difficulties within China's transportation sector.

The limiting words in this topic are 'China' and 'transportation sector'. Complete the following table with as many related words as possible. Example answers have been provided in the first row.

Transportation		Sector (Businesss)
a) Examples of...	b) Related ideas	c) What affects business?
High-speed railway	Fuel	Prices

By combining these words together (eg a + b + c), write down a range of possible search strings. Using a search engine, record how many results you can find for each search string. Location is also important, so add 'China', or one of its cities, to your search string for different results.

Search string	Results	Search string	Results
High-speed railway fuel prices	2,040,000		

Exercise 1

ℹ Judge the reliability of the following sources. Give reasons for your choices.

Authority (Who?)

For an essay with the title of *'challenges faced by environmentally friendly hotels'*, which of the following authors has the authority to discuss this topic?

Adventurous Dave

At age 28, I quit my job to travel the world alone. I have travelled to every continent on the planet (including Antartica!) and decided to set up this blog along the way to support my travel expenses. Six years later, I'm up to 75 countries, and still counting.

I have stayed in every kind of accommodation, from luxury five-star resorts, to hostels that cost a little as $1 per night. My goal is to show you, and the travel industry, what tourism really means.

Be sure to follow me, and don't miss out!

Dr. Jennifer Simmonds ✉

Jennifer Simmonds (PhD) is a senior lecturer in the School of Business at Lancaster University, where she teaches at undergraduate and postgraduate level. She has formerly taught at Imperial College Business School, where she was head of the faculty of Business. Her research interests include consumer behaviour, destination governance, and sustainable tourism.

She has published in Annals of Tourism Research, the Journal of Consumer Behaviour, Tourism Management, European Journal of Tourism, and Tourism Review. Her latest article in the Journal of Sustainable Tourism, entitled "The Theoretical Approach to Sustainable Tourism: issues of the 'new tourism'" has been highly praised as paving the way for substantial changes within the industry.

Currency (When?)

For a supporting point that is trying to highlight the *'devastating effects of the most recent job cuts across hospitals in the UK'*, which of the following articles will be most suitable?

NHS

Recent 'devastating' cuts places strain on London's hospitals

👤 **Denis Hopkins** 🕐 **22nd May 2018 @ 10:43AM**   ↗

Home > News > Health

Real effects of NHS job cuts revealed

More than 60,000 doctors, nurses, and midwives have lost their jobs in recent months, according to a recent survey of the health cuts. Promises broken by the government within their first year of power.

Richard Hart, Political Correspondent   13:18 26TH February 2011

....

....

Accuracy (Where?)

Look at the following three paragraphs; each taken from a different source. Decide which one should be used as evidence to demonstrate the *'number of people in the US that quit smoking during 2017'*.

a. Over the course of 2017, 4.5 per cent of smokers in the US managed to kick the habit, according to one government survey. This is an increase of 1.1 percent from the previous year, representing roughly an additional 350,000 smokers over the course of 12 months.

b. It is clear to see that in the past year, the amount of people smoking has severely decreased. When looking into the data, it is estimated that upwards of 40% of smokers have managed to quit. From those who were surveyed, it seemed to be the introduction of e-cigarettes that has led to this huge number of success stories.

c. According to the Centre of Disease Control and Prevention (2018), the percentage of smokers who managed to quit smoking rose from 3.4 to 4.5 percent between 2016 and 2017. A report from the Department of Health and Human Services (2018) interprets this data as "in 2016, nearly 21 out of every 100 adults were smokers", but in 2017 that number had decreased to "nearly 15 out of every 100 adults".

....

....

Objectivity (Why?)

Read the following two paragraphs. Decide which one would be considered more objective.

a. On average, people spend roughly 90 minutes a day poking away at their phones, and according to the study by Lepp et al. (2013), this leads to inferior aerobic fitness. Furthermore, Lepp et al. (2013) drew links between heavy phone use and insomnia. This is due to the light emitted from the phone screen unbalancing the sleep hormone melatonin. However, for all the adverse effects phones have on our health, they are also excellent tools for tracking and keeping us motivated. One study found that 82 per cent of recreational athletes relied on smartphone apps paired with fitness tech, with 75 per cent stating that the phone motivated them to work out (Bailey, 2016).

b. As a nation, are we getting lazier? Well, it would seem that way to most. Several studies have shown how we are wasting away hours while sitting on the sofa, flicking through our social media pages or playing the latest game that is all the rage right now. But it doesn't have to be that way! There are so many useful apps out there that will help you get up and running. FitnessPal, Results, Lifesum, and Nike+ all provide you with a variety of workout plans, all of which are proven to help any user get back into shape.

....

....

....

....

8.2 – Skimming and scanning

Exercise 1

ⓘ Use the article *'International student support'* to answer the following questions. Where possible, use your own words (ie do not copy exact phrases/sentences from the article).

a. How do pre-arrival programmes support international students?

....

....

b. Why are international students invited to attend orientation a week earlier?

....

....

c. What does the University of Warwick do to help welcome international students?

....

....

d. What unique activities does the University of Canberra offer during their orientation?

....

....

Exercise 2

ℹ Locate the following words in the article *'International student support'*. Write down the paragraph number and in which line the word can be located (eg the word 'settle' can be located in P2 L2).

Accustomed	Anxiety	Bearings	Befriend	Designated	Emotional	Explicit
P__ L__	P__ L__	P__ L__	P__ L__	P__ L__	P__ L__	P__ L__
Ignorant	Registering	System	Tournament	Tuition	Vital	Volunteers
P__ L__	P__ L__	P__ L__	P__ L__	P__ L__	P__ L__	P__ L__

International student support

1) The exciting experience of studying abroad is packed with opportunity and wonder. However, for the first few months, it may also be filled with anxiety and mental strain from having to acclimatise to such a different environment. This is brought on by moving to a new country, with an unfamiliar language and culture, while leaving your parents and friends behind and suddenly finding yourself quite literally being surrounded by strangers. On top of all this, you will have to get accustomed to an entirely new form of education, complete with a new set of rules and teachers.

2) Universities all over the world are not ignorant of this; on the contrary, they are setting numerous programmes to help international students settle in their new lives as smoothly as possible.

3) The most common programme in place at almost any university that enrols international students is the pre-arrival support. This is a set of vital information to get you started, like how to arrange medical insurance, tuition fee payments, visa requirements, and how to secure a bed on campus. Essentially, all you need to know to prepare for a comfortable and safe arrival. Although this seems quite basic, it ensures students hit the ground running.

4) Most universities follow up on this with an orientation programme aimed at international students. They usually hold them a week in advance, so the campus is not overwhelmingly crowded, and proceed to pack this week with activities that will offer both practical and emotional support. Take for example the University of Warwick; they have put together a programme that offers international students a few days of campus tours, accommodation lectures and social events where they can meet and befriend other students from around the world.

5) Some other universities have gone above and beyond with their orientation weeks. For example, the University of Canberra in Australia offers a boat and bus tour, a team race around the campus and even a football tournament addressed exclusively at international students, with the explicit aim of helping them adjust to their new home.

English for Academic Purposes: A Handbook for Students

6) *The practical aspect of these orientation programmes often includes tutorials centred around setting up bank accounts or registering for your new resident country's health care system.*

7) *Because the first few months are by far the hardest in an international student's life when it comes to finding their bearings, the majority of faculty support is focused at this initial stage. This does not mean, however, that there are no ongoing support programmes for international students. Almost all universities have a programme where faculty members or student volunteers are part of a Support Team which is available to International students at all times. They might encounter problems along their studies that will overwhelm them, like homesickness or health problems. In these cases, they have the email address and phone number of a designated Support Team member they can contact at any time.*

8.3 – SQ3R

Exercise 1

ⓘ While reading the article *'Reasons for Nokia's decline'*, use the SQ3R method of reading to measure your understanding.

Survey

Start by reading the title, headings, first paragraph, and the final paragraph. Based on this information, predict four things you will learn from reading this article in more detail.

1) ....

2) ....

3) ....

4) ....

Question

Based on your predictions, write down four questions you need to find the answer to.

1) ....

2) ....

3) ....

4) ....

Read

Now read the article and look for answers to the questions you have written above. If you find any useful information or keywords, highlight or underline them.

Record

After each section or paragraph, make some notes (you may need to use your notebook for this stage). Write a brief summary of each paragraph: the main ideas, any claims that have been made, any data or statistics, and any other important details (such as names, locations and dates).

Review

Finally, review your four questions and the notes you have made. Did you manage to answer all your questions? If so, this means you have a strong ability to judge an article during the surveying stage. Use this strength while researching to identify which sources are useful before reading them in detail.

Reasons for Nokia's decline

Many renowned companies have failed in the past. The failure or downfall of the mighty Nokia, which once led the mobile phone industry and ruled for almost 14 years, was primarily due to some costly mistakes that resulted in them losing the battle.

Smart competitors

Ten years ago, Nokia's phones were iconic, and everyone felt proud to carry these little gadgets. At this time, Nokia had the largest market share, but the company simply basked in their existing glory and did not evolve with its competitors. Companies like Samsung produced innovative technologies while Nokia lagged in the race. Samsung entered from nowhere and snatched sales to become the number one mobile phone distributor. It did everything right starting from innovations in their OS to its phone's physical design.

Lack of innovation

Every year both Samsung and Apple updated their products with a new innovative model with not only better specs but also a sleeker design. Nokia tried to adapt to this method by introducing the Lumia and N-series but failed to attract customers back from its competitors.

Lacks ecosystem

On a global scale, smartphones are the most popular gadgets. Therefore, they must be able to share and transfer content between devices. Google and Apple each have their own robust ecosystems. However, even after the few benefits gained by Nokia's acquisition of Microsoft's ecosystem, the company inherently did not gain anything in comparison to its competitors.

Although its Lumia 900 model won best in show award and its appearance was admired by many, the lack of a proper ecosystem was Nokia's biggest downfall. Many favourite apps found on Android and iOS were not downloadable in Microsoft's store. This further resulted in users shifting drastically towards Android and the iPhone.

English for Academic Purposes: A Handbook for Students

Complacency

As Nokia was a market leader for more than a decade, the company did not plan for the future, but instead it took pride in its existing products. When the first iPhone was launched in 2007, Nokia believed its E-series was a suitable competitor. However, the meaning of smartphone was beginning to change. At first, the iPhone's success did not drastically affect Nokia, but Samsung played with new enthralling technologies and transitioned faster than any other company. Nokia failed to do so and remained complacent.

The moral of this story is: to remain a successful market leader, businesses must evolve with their competitors, and continue to think outside of the box. The business world is a place of uncertainty and trends are changing continuously.

Exercise 1

ⓘ Compare the original sentence and the example paraphrases. Identify which one is well paraphrased, and which is an example of plagiarism. Explain your reasoning.

Original: 'New home prices jumped 1.3 per cent month over month in August, the strongest increase since 2011, according to data from JPMorgan' (Sender, 2016).

Paraphrase 1: According to research from JPMorgan, new home prices rose 1.3 per cent month over month in August, which was the strongest increase since 2011 (Sender, 2016).

Notes

....

....

....

Paraphrase 2: A JPMorgan report highlighted that from July to August there was an increase of 1.3 percent in the cost of newly built homes, and that such a significant change had not occurred in the past five years (Sender, 2016).

Notes

....

....

....

Exercise 2

ℹ Read the original sentences, and then decide which of the following options are closest in meaning.

Original 1

'From 2000 to 2015, the number of out-of-school children of lower secondary school age shrank from 97 million to 62 million' (UNICEF, 2018).

a. 62 million students are secondary school dropouts.

b. Since 2000, there has been a huge decrease in the number of children absent from secondary school.

c. The number of children missing out on a secondary school education had decreased by 35 million between 2000 and 2015.

Original 2

'There were 76,054 four-hour delays from decision to admit to admission this month, which compares to 42,970 in the same month last year' (NHS, 2018).

a. 76,054 people had to wait four hours to see a doctor.

b. In comparison to last year, there had been an increase of roughly 77 per cent in the number of people having to wait four hours to receive medical treatment.

c. Over the course of one year, there has been a steady increase of 33,084 patients needing to wait four hours or more to see a doctor.

Original 3

'Barnes & Noble [...] saw its stock price plunge nearly 8% just days after the New York Times published an editorial calling for the chain to be saved' (Helmore, 2018).

a. In the days following the release of an article by the New York Times, the market value of Barnes & Noble decreased by almost 8 per cent.

b. The New York Times are to blame for Barnes & Noble's loss of value.

c. The 8 per cent decrease in Barnes & Noble's stock price was the result of an article pleading for their support.

Exercise 3

ⓘ Attempt to paraphrase the following sentences. Remember to follow the steps outlined in Unit 9.2.

a. *'Ironically, the more consumers depend on their smartphones, the more they seem to suffer from their presence – or, more optimistically, the more they may stand to benefit from their absence'* (Ward et al., 2017).

....

....

....

....

b. *'For example, individuals with certain health conditions may find it useful to connect over social media, especially if they are geographically isolated'* (Primack et al., 2017).

....

....

....

....

c. *'The online learning setting, compared to a traditionally instructional one, allows students much more freedom in self-expression and flexibility in instant response to peers at all times and everywhere'* (Ekahitanond, 2017).

....

....

....

....

d. *'In recent years, vandalism has emerged as a significant threat to information quality and trustworthiness of collaborative social media application such as Wikipedia'* (Ramaswamy et al., 2014).

....

....

....

....

9.3 – Summarising

Exercise 1

🛈 Read and make notes on the following extracts. Using your notes of the main ideas presented, write a separate summary for each extract. **NOTE:** Do not look at the original extract while writing your summary (eg cover it with a piece of paper); otherwise you may be tempted to copy.

Extract 1

Since almost every person in the civilised world has a smartphone in their pockets, we have come to expect this reality to be the standard, forgetting that only 150 years ago the very notion of the telephone was non-existent. Contrary to what most people believe, it was not Alexander Graham Bell who invented the first telephone, but Antonio Meucci, an Italian. Bell, living in America and working on his invention, wholly unaware and separate from Meucci, was awarded a patent for the telephone 7 March 1876. With his invention recognised, things began to flourish, and the Bell Telephone Company was set up in the following year. Bell owned a third of the shares, thus becoming a wealthy man and more importantly, sealing his name as the inventor of the telephone in popular culture forever. We have come a long way since you had to be extremely rich to be able to afford a landline telephone in your home, with today's devices going completely mobile.

Author: *Calin Barnes, 21 May 2018*

Extract 2

Image capturing was traced back to the early 1800s, with partially successful attempts at capturing fixed images registered in 1816. It took roughly 150 years to evolve from that to the early stages of the digital camera we are all familiar with today. It started with conceptual work in the early 1960s and 1970s done by Eugene Lally of Jet Propulsion Laboratory and Willis Adcock of Texas Instruments, but reached the masses when Nikon introduced the first digital single-lens reflex (DSLR) in 1986. Another ten years had to pass through until it became common among consumers in the second half of the 1990s, which makes for just 20 years between the moment people embraced the digital camera to where we are today. In just 20 years we have gone from bulky cameras with an inferior quality of image capturing and prices to match a luxury item to something that is completely common and affordable.

Author: *Calin Barnes, 21 May 2018*

9.5 – Quotations

Exercise 1

ⓘ Using the article *'Exposé of the fashion industry'*, write a suitable quotation for the following points.

Supporting points

a. The fashion industry has adopted the idea of 'fast fashion' for several reasons.

....

....

b. These poor working conditions have led to horrific accidents.

....

....

c. Furthermore, the fashion industry blindly ignores the use of child labour.

....

....

d. Additionally, these workshops encourage the practice of 'soft slavery'.

....

....

e. Owners of these factories and workshops blame the retailers for their problems.

....

....

Exercise 2

ⓘ As an overuse of quotations is usually avoided in academic writing, attempt to paraphrase the quotations you chose to use in support of the points in *Exercise 1*.

....

....

....

....

....

....

....

Exposé of the fashion industry

Popular culture today has grown into a monster of consumption. This behaviour applies to anything from information to food. For example, household items always get replaced with better tech in a matter of a few years. Everything these days seems to be built to please, but not to last. This practice is most evident in the fashion industry that has embraced extensively over the years what is referred to as 'fast fashion'. It is the current craze of bringing the latest trends from the catwalk as soon as possible and as affordable as can be. Colossal fashion retailers implement this to boost sales and keep their clients entertained. In a world where entitlement and desire are prevalent, there is no time to waste if a business wants to make money. They keep clients spending by catering to their ridiculously fast-changing tastes and whims.

Unfortunately, there are no free rides in life, so one's benefit comes at another's expense. Although huge brand names such as Zara or H&M are implementing fast fashion in their business models, there have been numerous whistle-blowers that have tried to expose the horrible conditions behind the manufacturing curtain. Most of these clothing types are created in either Bangladesh or India, with horrible working conditions and large-scale pollution. In recent history, there was a horrific accident in Savar, Bangladesh, when 1,134 people died due to structural failure in a garments factory. This incident drew more attention to the industry's shady manufacturing policies, and is to date the deadliest structural failure accident in modern history and a clear-cut example of hideous practices. Hobson's (2013) report details that the bank and the shops on the ground floor immediately closed when cracks were discovered in the building's walls, while the workers in the garment factory were ordered back to work the following day. The building then collapsed at rush hour, claiming the lives of the workers who were threatened to have their monthly pay withheld if they did not enter the building to work.

Other repeatedly reported problems include: child labour, as according to UNICEF (2017), over 150 million children are working in the fashion manufacturing industry worldwide, and a form of soft slavery where workers are kept indebted to third parties for securing them jobs in garment factories. What happens is that they end up giving away most of their small earnings to pay off that debt that will never end. For an industry that is said to be worth 3 trillion dollars (Woodyard, 2017), all these problems are completely unacceptable. The factory owners themselves are under significant pressure from the retailers, as they demand faster production times and lower prices, forcing factories to work with the worst materials and a lack of care for the manufacturing process. This results in clothes that last but a few months or sometimes only days before they need replacing.

The fashion industry has evolved into a consumption machine unrivalled by any other industry except, probably, the food industry. It is an ego-driven consumption race for a social statement on one side and growing profits on the other. Nothing in life comes free, and the bill for our indulgence is paid in blood, sweat and tears by the workers in garment factories.

Author: *Calin Barnes, 14 April 2018*

Exercise 1

🛈 In the following sentences, choose which reporting verb could be used to replace 'said' or 'stated'. The verb should accurately convey the correct purpose and strength.

a. The department managers stated that reducing the number of staff members would compromise customer satisfaction levels.

Accepted	Revealed	Warned

b. In response to the recent oil spill, BP says that the damage to the local wildlife is minimal and actions are being taken to restore their natural habitat.

Recommends	Stresses	Reasons

c. A report from UNICEF states that one in five children are without access to education.

Advises	Estimates	Promises

d. Researchers stated that people who drink three cups of coffee a day are more likely to develop cases of insomnia.

Discovered	Uphold	Admitted

e. The National Union of Students (NUS) says that increased tuition fees are resulting in a reduction of students from low-income families applying for university.

Imagines	Urges	Argues

f. Many large automotive companies stated that battery-powered motors would replace the current combustion engine. However, things began to change when Tesla entered the market.

Hoped	Doubted	Guaranteed

10.2 – Citations

Exercise 1

ⓘ Identify what errors occur in the following citations

a. According to **Smith, Jones, Lewis, Lane, and Michael (2014)**, the…

b. …a sizable benefit for users (**Ryan, 2017 and Osmond, 2018**).

c. **Liss (2016, as cited in West, 2011)** commented that…

d. …career can continue at full pace (**Timothy Laidler, 2016**).

e. **No name (2011)** suggested that businesses…

f. …for a significant majority of the students (**Hambly**).

g. **Graham, D. (2017)** argued that nothing is more important…

h. …first line of defence for an athlete's health (**McKinlay etc. 2013**).

10.3 – Reference lists

Exercise 1

ⓘ Rewrite the following reference list entries into their correct order.

a. *The innovator's dilemma*, Christensen, C. M. New York: Harper Collins. (2003)

....

b. Cox, C. K. 'Tertiary level writing', (1993) 12 (1) pp. 52–60. *EA Journal*,

....

c. Available at: (Accessed: 25 March 2010). *Are games better than life?* www.ted.com/talks/david_perry_on_videogames (2006) Perry, D.

....

....

d. [PowerPoint Presentation]. Morgan, C. *Sustainable practice* (2017) Available at: *SSP7057: Sustainable Tourism*. (Accessed: 11 November 2017). www.ucm.ac.uk/resources/2017-11-09/sustainable-practice-ppt

....

....

Exercise 2

ℹ️ Look at these sources. First, identify what type of source is being presented, and then highlight the information needed to write a reference list.

Next, write a complete reference list for all six sources. Remember to write them in the correct order.

Source 1

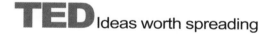

TEDWomen 2017 | November 2017   1,815,222 views

Lera Borodisky - Cognitive scientist

How language shapes the way we think

https://www.ted.com/talks/lera_boroditsky_how_language_shapes_the_way_we_think

Source 2

THE STUDY SKILLS HANDBOOK
STELLA COTTRELL
FOURTH EDITION

First Edition 1999
Second Edition 2003
Third Edition 2008
Fourth Edition 2013

Palgrave Macmillan
Houndsmill
Baisingstoke
Hampshire
RG21 6XS

Source 3

Office for
National Statistics

3 January 2018

trade@ons.gsi.gov.uk

Who does the UK trade with?

https://www.ons.gov.uk/businessindustryandtrade/internationaltrade/
articles/whodoestheuktradewith/2017-02-21

Source 4

Vol. 32, Issue 4
(December 2017)

Journal of
Information Technology

Open the floodgates: the implications of increasing platform openness in crowdfunding

Michael Wessel, Ferdinand Thies, Alaxander Benlian

Pages 344-360   https://doi.org/10.1057/s41265-017-0040-z

Source 5

Accounting Comparability, Audit Effort, and Audit Outcomes

Joseph H. Zhang

CONTEMPORARY
ACCOUNTING
RESEARCH

Volume 35, Issue 1
Spring 2018
Pages 245-276

https://doi.org/10.1111/1911-3846.12381

Source 6

Management Across Cultures

Developing Global Competencies

THIRD EDITION
September 2016

Cambridge University Press
University Printing House
Cambridge, CB2 8BS

Richard M. Steers
Luciara Nardon
Carlos J. Sanchez-Runde

11.2 – Improving cohesion

Exercise 1

ℹ️ **Revise the following sentences using coordinating conjunctions.**

   a. The company was losing money. They decided to sell some of their assets.

   ....

   b. Researchers claimed they gathered enough data. The sample size was too small.

   ....

   c. Their product was not innovative. It was also not priced competitively.

   ....

   d. Perhaps the event failed because of the weather. Perhaps it was the inaccessible location.

   ....

Exercise 2

ℹ️ **Revise the following sentences using subordinating conjunctions.**

   a. Technology offers many benefits. It can also cause some difficulties.

   ....

   b. Some employees require careful guidance. Others are far more independent.

   ....

   c. The student finished her work early. She had time for her tutor to provide feedback.

   ....

d. Samsung has steadily increased its share in the smartphone market. Nokia's share has rapidly decreased.

....

e. Inflation is rising. The national average wage has not increased.

....

11.3 – Proofreading

Exercise 1

ⓘ Identify the errors in the following paragraphs. There are 20 mistakes in total, with the number in brackets indicating how many errors are contained within each paragraph.

Advice for proofreading

Proofreading your work is quite essential, as even professional writers make mistake in they earlier drafts. Many writers believe their word processing software will identify all the errors as they writing, and that proofreading in an unnecessary process. However, even the best spelling and grammar checking software can overlook obvious some mistakes. Therefore, it is important to review any written work armed with some revision Proofreading techniques. (5)

First, reading an text out loud can help, as this forces the writer to the focus on every single word. Silently reeding a paper will often lead to rushing through and self-correcting any errors within the brain. Reading backwards will also direct the attention to each word, as the grammar and context are removed. this method is especially usefully when checking for spelling mistakes. (4)

Focusing on once sentence at a time can also reduce the risk of reading too quickly. This can also be achieved by reading backwards. Start with the last

(continued overleaf)

sentence in the paper, then move on to the previous sentence. This should be repeated until the opening sentence of the paper has being reached. (3)

Checking for grammatical errorr is possibly the most challenging stage. Sometimes something will seem in of place, or there may be a case of uncertainty regarding situations where 'that' or 'which' could be used. Be prepare to do a little research by having a good grammar book ready to review any grammatical rules that cause confusion (4)

Using a hard copy (a printed version) will also be useful extremely, as this allows for marks (such as symbols and abbreviations) or notes to be made. Although word processing software does allow for notes, this cannot be a little more time-consuming. however, if proofreading is done on a computer, it does mean that immediate changes can be made. But, it also means that sometimes when one corrections is made quickly, another one may appear and then be overlooked. (4)

Exercise 1

ℹ Look at the following example of an essay. Identify which areas have been formatted incorrectly.

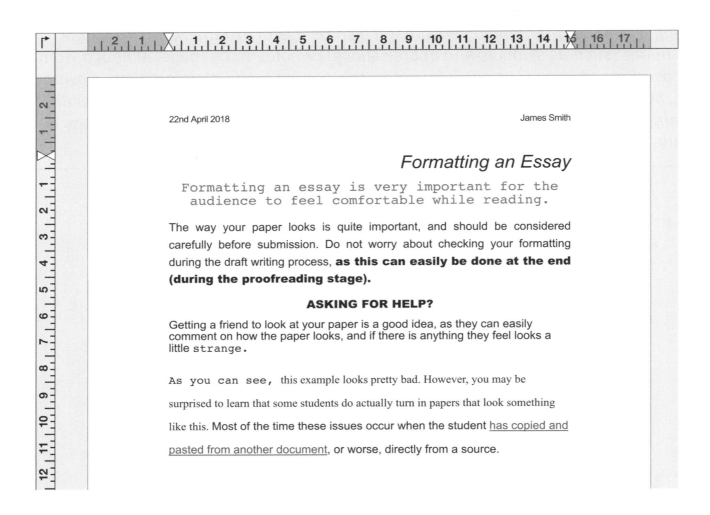

References

NOTE: Some of the texts/examples used in the exercise section are original or fictitious pieces used purely for the purpose of practice. Below are the reference details for all authentic texts used within the exercise section of this book:

Apple (no date) *App Review.* Available at: https://developer.apple.com/app-store/review (Accessed: 10 May 2018).

Bailey, M. (2016) 'Phones Update Your Health'. *Men's Health,* September, p. 41.

Biggs, J. and Tang, C. (2011) *Teaching for Quality Learning at University.* 4th edn. Maidenhead: McGraw-Hill Education.

Cohen, A. P., Azrael, D. and Miller, M. (2014) *Rate of Mass Shootings Has Tripled Since 2001, Harvard Research Shows.* Available at: https://developer.apple.com/app-store/review (Accessed: 13 May 2018).

Ekahitanond, V. (2017) 'Using LINE as a Platform for Encouraging Students' Learning and Participation'. *TEM Journal,* 6(4) pp. 832–838.

Foley, S., Karlsen, J. R. and Putniņš, T. J. (2018) *Sex, Drugs, and Bitcoin: How Much Illegal Activity Is Financed Through Cryptocurrencies?* Available at: www.law.ox.ac.uk/business-law-blog/blog/2018/02/sex-drugs-and-bitcoin-how-much-illegal-activity-financed-through (Accessed: 13 May 2018).

Helmore, E. (2018) *Barnes & Noble: Why It Could Soon be the Bookshop's Final Chapter.* Available at: www.theguardian.com/books/2018/may/12/barnes-noble-bookstores-retail-amazon (Accessed: 25 May 2018).

Hobson, J. (2013) 'To Die For? The Health and Safety of Fast Fashion'. *Occupational Medicine,* 63(5) pp. 317–319.

Lepp, A. et al. (2013) The Relationship Between Cell Phone Use, Physical and Sedentary Activity, and Cardiorespiratory Fitness in a Sample of U.S. College Students. *International Journal of Behavioral Nutrition and Physical Activity,* 10(79) pp. 1–9. doi: 10.1186/1479-5868-10-79.

Leswing, K. (2018) *Apple Just Shared Some Staggering Statistics About How Well the App Store is Doing (AAPL).* Available at: https://finance.yahoo.com/news/apple-just-shared-staggering-statistics-220301223.html (Accessed: 10 May 2018).

McCord, P. (2014) *How Netflix Reinvented HR.* Available at: https://hbr.org/2014/01/how-netflix-reinvented-hr (Accessed: 13 May 2018).

NHS (2018) *A&E Attendances and Emergency Admissions March 2018 Statistical Commentary.* Available at: www.england.nhs.uk/statistics/wp-content/uploads/sites/2/2018/04/Statistical-commentary-March-2018-uC145.pdf (Accessed: 25 May 2018).

Primack, B. A. et al. (2017) 'Social Media Use and Perceived Social Isolation Among Young Adults in the US', *American Journal of Preventive Medicine,* 53(1) pp. 1–8.

Ramaswamy, L. et al. (2014) 'Harnessing Context for Vandalism Detection in Wikipedia', *ICST Transactions on Collaborative Computing,* 14(1) pp. 1–14.

Sender, H. (2016) *China's Property Bulls Keep Running Hard.* Available at: www.ft.com/content/90ea7314-8acb-11e6-8aa5-f79f5696c731 (Accessed: 25 May 2018).

Statista (2018) *Number of Available Apps in the Apple App Store from July 2008 to January 2017.* Available at: www.statista.com/statistics/263795/number-of-available-apps-in-the-apple-app-store (Accessed: 10 May 2018).

UNICEF (2017) *Child Protection from Violence, Exploitation and Abuse: Child Labour.* [online] Available at: www.unicef.org/protection/57929_child_labour.html (Accessed: 25 May 2018).

UNICEF (2018) *Secondary Education: Current Status and Progress.* Available at: https://data.unicef.org/topic/education/secondary-education (Accessed: 25 May 2018).

Ward, A. F. et al. (2017) Brain Drain: The Mere Presence of One's Own Smartphone Reduces Available Cognitive Capacity. *Journal of the Association for Consumer Research,* 2(2) pp. 140–154.

Woodyard, P. (2017) *Fast Fashion's Effect on People, the Planet, & You.* Available at: www.youtube.com/watch?v=mPM9lhackHw (Accessed: 25 May 2018).

Zepke, N. and Leach, L. (2010) 'Improving Student Engagement: Ten Proposals for Action'. *Active Learning in Higher Education,* 11(3) pp. 167–177.